THE ESSENTIAL

Jim Carrey

An Unofficial
Fan Guide

M. A. Cassata

Other books by M. A. Cassata:

The Cher Scrapbook

The Elton John Scrapbook

'NSync

Britney Spears

Hey, Hey, We're The Monkees

Cher!

Michael J. Fox

The Essential Jim Carrey
© 2009 Mary Anne Cassata. All Rights Reserved.

Published in the USA by:
BearManor Media
P O Box 71426
Albany, Georgia 31708
www.bearmanormedia.com

ISBN 978-1-59393-517-7

Printed in the United States of America.

Disclaimer: This publication was not authorized or sponsored By Jim Carrey or any affiliate thereof.

Book and cover design by Darlene Swanson • www.van-garde.com

Contents

Part 3

Acknowledgements

A project as extensive as this has been years in the making: I was for-
tunate enough to come in contact with so many wonderful people that
have helped make this book possible. For starters, heartfelt thanks go
to Lisa Wagner, Anne Raso, Neil Wexler, Jamie Cassata, Daniel Zim-
merman and Ellen Kovarik for their unfailing assistance.

For those who have shared their admiration and support for Jim
Carrey and his films I will always be grateful. In particular I would like
to thank the Historica Foundation's William Beard, Paul Townsend and
Chantal Gagnon.

A special thanks to Darlene Swanson for her great work on making
all the crazy last minute changes. Also BearManor publisher Ben Ohm-
art for his kindness and understanding of how needed this book was for
the thousands of loyal and serious Jim Carrey fans worldwide.

As for the research, much was conducted at the New York City
Public Library for the Performing Arts at Lincoln Center and The Museum of Television and Public Radio in New York, as well as various
Internet sources including the Bergen County Cooperative Library System, and the members-only section of Internet Movie Database.

For those who openly shared their best Jim Carrey memories, personal collections, particularly you *Jim Carrey Online* fans — many of whom

didn't give me last names — my thanks go to you: Linda Alamprese, Marcia Tysseling, Priya Baboota, Christopher Van Espen (Belgium), Mandy, (England) Dan Rhodenizer, Laura Laing and Lynn (Canada), Happy Gal, Nicola West and Marcella (Italy), Joyce S, Robert F., Mark B., Daniel J., Anthony C., Staci L., William L., Cheryl N., Justin W., and Jack B.

For all the new friends I've met through the course of writing *The Essential Jim Carrey,* I thank each and every one of you for your generosity, encouragement and patience. A big tip of the hat goes to the ever dedicated and unfailing Jim Carrey Online staff (particularly Tommy Pihl), all of whom were so patient and accommodating with my never-ending barrage of questions and requests.

Finally, I would like to acknowledge Jim Carrey, the man himself, who inspires millions and never fails to make us smile.

PART 1

Introduction

> "I think it's important never to look a gift horse in
> the mouth and never to overlook your talents, what
> you're good at and so I really say it sounds like a
> great creative challenge to me. It doesn't matter
> whether it's dramatic or comedic."
>
> — Jim Carrey

Why did I write this book? I must be mad! The thought had entered my mind from time to time as I prepared these pages. After all, I screened more than 25 movies, dozens of *In Living Color* Jim Carrey snippets, and about 100 television appearances — all the while analyzing the how's and why's of Jim Carrey's popularity. As anyone who has ever followed his career knows, transforming his face on film is now a long standing Jim Carrey tradition.

I had the honor and privilege of speaking to Jim again while *Disney's A Christmas Carol* train tour made its final stop at Grand Central Station in New York City. While on the train with other members of the press, Jim promoted the film and the tour, which began back in May 2009 in Los Angeles and spanned more than 16,000 miles of track. The train tour featured behind-the-scenes of the movie Charles Dickens Museum artifacts, preview of the film in 3-D, concept art and costumes.

Always the funny man, Jim was all smiles as usual during the closing ceremony, dancing around, and stuffing confetti in his mouth for the cameras. To promote the film, he briefly discussed the awesome techniques that were used in the production. "The soul of the character is all you need," he offered to the press. "It's an actor driven media and an amazing process, the muscles in my face are driving these dots. It's a fascinating process."

It's hard not to think about the other Christmas movie Jim Carrey is famous for, playing yet another meanie—*How the Grinch Stole Christmas*. Jim even joked that, "They seem to drag me out at Christmas time, I'm a kind of snow plough."

So, in any case, the main purpose of *The Essential Jim Carrey* is to celebrate the life and career of this man— an enormous talent, who has inspired people, including myself, through laughter and instilled a sense of hope with his acting craft. Whether you are a new fan, or an old one, these pages will connect you with one of most beloved actors of our generation and give you a greater appreciation of his true genius. It is my fondest wish that fans of Jim Carrey will read this book and be as inspired by him as I have been over the years.

—M. A. Cassata
January 2010

Dedicated to Jim Carrey's artistry.

Part 1

CHAPTER 1

Why We Love Jim Carrey

He's been the major force behind some of the best and memorable comedies of all time. Not only has he won over the hearts of loyal fans from around the world for his comedic work, Jim Carrey has also earned the respect of the Hollywood elite and critics for his powerhouse performances in such dramatic films as *Man on the Moon*, *The Truman Show*. *The Majestic* and *Eternal Sunshine of the Spotless Mind*. At this writing, Carrey was being praised for his lead character voice-over in the animated feature, *Dr. Seuss' Horton Hears a Who*, and (though not confirmed) is expected to star as Robert Ripley in Tim Burton's *Ripley's Believe It, Or Not*.

Often compared to comedic legends such as Jerry Lewis, Robin Williams and Charlie Chaplin, Carrey's trademark elastic face and bizarre slapstick humor have charmed millions of fans from around world and at the same time sent his films to the top of the box office charts

Many would agree that there has never been an actor equally hilarious and moving. He has made us laugh, and occasionally cry, as Ace Ventura, Bruce Nolan, Stanley Ipkiss, Fletcher Reed, Dick Harper, The Grinch and Count Olaf.

In reality, Jim Carrey proves more of a modern clown man, who can equally portray both the comic and the tragic. Perhaps it's his more recent movies that tend to blur the line between comedy and tragedy. Either way, it looks like Jim Almighty has found a balance between the best of both film worlds and his loyal following wouldn't have it any other way.

CHAPTER 2

The Jim Carrey Basics

At a Glance

Stage Name: Jim Carrey

Also Known as: James Carrey

Born: January 17, 1962

Birth Name: James Eugene Carrey

Horoscope Sign: Capricorn

Birth Place: Newmarket, Ontario, Canada

Nick Names: Jimmy-Gene The String Bean

Parents' Names: (Father) Percy (saxophonist, clarinetist, accountant); (Mother) Kathleen (homemaker)

Siblings: Two older sisters: Patricia and Rita and one older brother: John

Religion: Raised Catholic; currently Presbyterian

Nationality: Born Canadian, Naturalized U.S. Citizen (2004)

Height: 6' 2"

Weight: Approximately 180 pounds

Eyes: Brown

Hair Color: Brown

Shoe Size: 11

Pets: Dogs; used to have an Iguana named Houston

Last Reported Favorite Book: Crime and Punishment by Fyodor Dostoevsky

Current Favorite Book Themes: Metaphysical, philosophy and self-help themes.

Education: Aldershot High School in Burlington, Ontario, Canada; Agincourt Collegiate Institute in Agincourt, Ontario, Canada (dropped out)

Profession: Actor, Comic, Screenwriter, Producer, and Musician

Early Inspirations: His father; comedians: Dick Van Dyke, Carol Burnett, Jimmy Stewart, Richard Pryor, and Robin Williams

First Stand Up Debut: 1977: Yuk Yuk's club in Toronto

Martial Status: Lauren Holly (actress; married on September 23, 1996; divorced on July 29, 1997), Melissa Womer (married on March 28, 1987; divorced in November 1993).

Children: One Daughter: Jane Erin Carrey (with Melissa Womer)

Dated Linda Ronstadt in 1984. Renee Zellweger, (met during filming of Me, Myself and Irene (December 1999-2000; separated), and Jenny McCarthy (2006-April 2010).

Favorites

Color: Green

Food: Grilled cheese sandwiches dipped in ketchup and Mexican food (as reported early in his career).

Music: Alternative Rock—Nirvana, Pearl Jam, Tom Petty, Green Day, Nine Inch Nails, The White Stripes, Cannibal Corpse, or "anything that sounds good."

Comedians: Dick Van Dyke, Jerry Lewis, Steve Martin, Rodney Dangerfield

Artists: Salvador Dali

Drinks: Diet Coke, red wine, bottled water

Charities: Comic Relief and Make-A-Wish Foundation. (Honorary Chairman) National Veterans Foundation (NVF)

Hobbies: Painting, sculpting, reading, singing, songwriting

Cars: First was Lexus; Current known is 1965 Thunderbird Convertible

Claim To Fame: Billed as James Carrey in the TV show *In Living Color* (1990)

Currently Resides: Malibu and Brentwood, CA

Production Company: JC 23 Entertainment (Producer)

Previous Company Names: Jimmy-Gene Inc. and Pit Bull Productions

Recorded Songs: "Somebody To Love," "Cuban Pete," "Grinch 2000," "You're A Mean One Mr. Grinch," "I Am the Walrus"

Songwriting: To date, one song, "Heaven Down Here" (1994), recorded by Folk/Rock artists Tuck and Patti

Where To Write:

Jim Carrey

P. O. Box: 57593

Sherman Oaks, CA 91403

Official Website: Jimcarrey.com

Official Twitter Page: Twitter.com/Jimcarrey

CHAPTER 3

Jim Carrey –
Brief Biographical Overview

James Eugene Carrey, "Jim," actor (born in Newmarket, Ontario January 17, 1962).

Jim Carrey, perhaps the most successful of the Canadian comic actors who have gone to Hollywood and made good, left a heavy imprint on American film comedy in the 1990s. His almost frighteningly manic attack, his gymnastically rubber face and his boundless appetite for excess go well beyond the limits of his predecessors. His characters swing wildly between the poles of monstrously fatuous pride and hysterical self-abasement, between sadistic megalomania and masochistic abjection.

He has been compared to Jerry Lewis in his willingness — even eagerness — to embarrass himself and others and to enact a manic-depressive crisis of self-worth in hyperkinetic comic terms. It is doubly ironic and appropriately incongruous that Carrey's uncontained and infantile spasms are performed by a body that is tall, muscular and even physically heroic (which can pass unnoticed, so powerful is the actor's will to the grotesque). His appetite for extremes of plasticity has led him (and in this he is in tune with the times) to the action cinema of fantasy and special effects, where his innate immoderation can be enhanced through animation, stunts and other cinematic tricks — most clearly seen in *The Mask* (1994).

After dropping out of high school to help his family at a time of financial crisis, he turned a childhood appetite for performance into a career as a teenage standup comic at the Yuk Yuk's club in Toronto. In 1981, when he was 19, he moved permanently to Los Angeles and worked as a standup comedian (at the Comedy Store), in series television —The Duck Factory (1984) and In Living Color (1990-94) — and in movie bit parts. In 1994, his career exploded with starring appearances in three hit movies: The Mask, Dumb and Dumber and Ace Ventura: Pet Detective. The following year came Batman Forever and Ace Ventura: When Nature Calls. His arrival was so loud and sudden that within a single month in 1995 he was featured on the covers of both Newsweek and Rolling Stone. In 1996 he received a startling $20 million fee to star in The Cable Guy, which failed to be the surefire hit it was supposed to be and drew comments that it was too "dark" to be funny. He followed this in 1997 with another typical Carrey film, Liar Liar, and then played against type with the offbeat, popular and critical successful The Truman Show (1998), in which he played a man gradually becoming aware that his whole life is displayed on a TV show watched by millions.

By this point in his career, Carrey could choose his projects with complete freedom. After an acclaimed appearance as comedian Andy Kaufman in Man on the Moon (1999), and as a man with multiple personalities in the manic comedy Me, Myself and Irene (2000), came the sentimental neo-Capra epic The Majestic (2001). It was a critical and box-office failure; however, the release of Dr Seuss' How the Grinch Stole Christmas (2000), with Carrey in the central role of the Grinch, grossed over $260 million, making it the biggest hit of his career to date.

The Grinch was followed by Bruce Almighty (2003), the critically acclaimed Eternal Sunshine of the Spotless Mind (2004), Lemony Snicket's A Series of Unfortunate Events (2004), Fun with Dick and Jane (2005), and the thriller The Number 23 (2007).

Jim Carrey has won six Golden Globes, 22 MTV Movie Awards (the most by any celebrity in MTV history), a Screen Actors Guild Award for *Man on the Moon*, and two People's Choice Awards. He was inducted into Canada's Walk of Fame in 1998. With an accumulative box-office gross in excess of $2 billion, he is without doubt the most powerful and influential Canadian-born actor working in Hollywood since Mary Pickford's reign as queen of the American cinema during the 1920s.

Throughout his career, Jim Carrey has always tried to improve his performance skills. In 2008 he made the Most Improved Actor list. Not many Hollywood actors can effortlessly transform from slapstick comedy to straight-in-your-face drama the way Carrey has exhibited since the mid-1990s. Who would have believed that the same rubber-faced dimwit in *Dumb and Dumber* could pull off one of the best dramatic performances of 2004 in *Eternal Sunshine of the Spotless Mind?* Even with *The Truman Show* and *The Majestic*, one could easily see the actor's flair for dramatic acting.

It also comes as no surprise that Jim Carrey ranks as one of the top Canadians of all time (a list that includes Mike Myers, Michael J. Fox and William Shatner), if not one of *the* most powerful, according to the acclaimed *Canadian Business Magazine*. The Number One spot went to John Candy. Jim Carrey became an American Citizen in 2004 in order to vote in American elections. In a statement he said: "This country has helped define me and make my dreams come true."

However, he has also maintained his Canadian citizenship. "I have no intention of giving up my Canadian heritage, and all those who loved and supported me. My upbringing in Canada made me the person I am."

— Reprinted with kind permission from William Beard,
revised by Paul Townend,
The Canadian Encyclopedia
Historia. All Rights Reserved.

CHAPTER 4

The Films of Jim Carrey

The information listing begins with his most recent projects and runs backwards, so you can see how far the award-winning actor has progressed in the often unpredictable, yet fantastic world of movie making. All Jim Carrey's films are now available on DVD; many are starting to appear on Blu-ray. See also Appendix 3 for a comprehensive filmography.

Films In Development (as of late-2009)
Working Title: *Damn Yankees*
Plot Summary: A modern-day take on the hit Broadway musical about a guy who makes a deal with the devil in order to see his favorite baseball team become champs.

Director: Todd Graff
Projected Theatrical Release: 2012

Major Theatrical Releases
Working Title: *Ripley's Believe It or Not*
Plot Summary: *Believe It or Not* picks up with Ripley at the time when he gained celebrity status through a "Believe it or Not" column that chronicled his search for the greatest oddities in the world.

Director: Scott Alexander

Projected Theatrical Release: 2011

I Love You Phillip Morris

Plot Summary: Fact-based story of a married man whose exploits find him in a Texas prison where he falls madly in love with his cellmate. When the cellmate is eventually released, Russell escapes from prison to be with him.

Director: Glenn Ficarra

Additional Cast: Ewan McGregor, Leslie Mann

A Christmas Carol (2009)

Plot Summary: Adaptation of the Charles Dickens tale of Ebenezer Scrooge and the three ghosts that haunt him: the Ghost of Christmas Past, the Ghost of Christmas Present and the Ghost of Christmas Future.

Director: Robert Zemeckis

Additional Cast: Gary Oldman, Colin Firth

Yes Man (2008)

Plot Summary: A divorcee decides to change his life when he says "yes" for one year to new opportunities he would normally turn down. Based on the memoir by Danny Wallace.

Director: Peyton Reed

Additional Cast: Zooey Dedschanel, Bradley Cooper

Horton Hears a Who! (2008)

Plot Summary: An imaginative elephant struggles to protect a micro-scopic community from his friends and neighbors who don't believe it actually exists.

Directors: Jimmy Hayward, Steve Martino

Additional Cast: Steve Carell, Carol Burnett, Seth Rogen

The Number 23 (2007)
Plot Summary: A man becomes obsessed with a novel that appears to be about his life. As his obsession grows stronger, numerous similarities seem to arise.

Director: Joel Schumacher

Additional Cast: Virginia Madsen, Logan Lerman, Danny Huston

Fun with Dick and Jane (2005)
Plot Summary: Remake of the 1977 comedy about a high-powered executive who loses his job. When he can't find work, he and his wife team up as armed robbers to keep their family together and make ends meets.

Additional Cast: Tea Leoni, Alec Baldwin, Richard Jenkins, Angie Harmon, John Michael Higgins

Lemony Snicket's A Series of Unfortunate Events (2004)
Plot Summary: Three wealthy children's parents perish in a fire. When they are sent to live with Count Olaf, a distant relative, they find out that he is plotting to kill them and inherit their fortune. This reduces the children's lives to an ever-reoccurring series of unfortunate events.

Director: Brad Silberling

Additional Cast: Liam Aiken, Emily Browning, Kara/Shelby Hoffman, Timothy Spall, Catherine O'Hara, Billy Connolly, Meryl Streep

Eternal Sunshine of the Spotless Mind (2004)
Plot summary: A couple comprised of polar opposites undergoes a procedure to erase each other from their memories when their relationship sours. But it is only through the process of loss that they discover what they had to begin with.

Director: Michel Gondry

Additional Cast: Kate Winslet, Elijah Wood, Kirsten Dunst, Tom Wilkenson

Bruce Almighty (2003)

Plot Summary: A TV newsman from Buffalo complains to God one too many times, and is endowed with almighty powers to teach him how difficult it is to run the world.

> Director: Tom Shadyac
>
> Additional Cast: Morgan Freeman, Jennifer Aniston, Philip Baker
>   Hall, Steven Carnell

The Majestic (2001)

Plot summary: A blacklisted 1951 Hollywood screenwriter gets into a car accident, loses his memory and settles down in a small town where he is mistaken for a long, lost son.

> Director: Frank Darabont
>
> Additional Cast: Bob Balaban, Jeffrey DeMunn, Hal Holbrook,
>   Laurie Holden, Martin Landau

Dr. Suess's How The Grinch Stole Christmas (2000)

Plot summary: A big-budget adaptation of the much-loved classic holiday Dr. Suess cartoon about a creature intent on stealing Christmas.

> Director: Ron Howard
>
> Additional Cast: Taylor Momsen, Jeffrey Tambor,
>   Christine Baranski, Bill Irwin

Me, Myself & Irene (2000)

Plot summary: A good guy Rhode Island officer with a multiple personality disorder escorts a fugitive woman back to her hometown. Along the way he and his alter-ego fall in love with her.

> Director: Bobby Farrelly
>
> Additional Cast: Renee Zellweger, Anthony Anderson,
>   Mongo Brownlee

Man on the Moon (1999)

Plot summary: A film about the life and career of Andy Kaufman, one of the most eccentric avant-garde comedian/actors of his time.

>Director: Milos Forman

>Additional Cast: Gerry Becker, Greyson Pendry, Brittany Colonna,
>>Danny DeVito, Leslie Lyles

Simon Birch (1998)

Plot summary: A young boy with stunted growth is convinced that God has a great purpose for him.

>Director: Mark Steven Johnson

>Additional Cast: Ian Michael Smith, Ashley Judd, Oliver Platt,
>>David Strathaim

The Truman Show (1998)

Plot summary: An insurance agent discovers his entire life is actually a TV show that has been running 24 hours a day since the day he was born.

>Director: Peter Weir

>Additional Cast: Laura Linney, Noah Emmerich, Natascha Taylor,
>>Brian Deleate

Liar Liar (1997)

Plot summary: A fast track lawyer can't lie for 24 hours due to his son's birthday wish, after the lawyer turns his son down for the last time.

>Director: Tom Shadyac

>Additional Cast: Maura Tierney, Justin Cooper, Cary Elwes,
>>Anne Haney

The Cable Guy (1996)

Plot summary: A lonely and emotional disturbed cable guy raised on television just wants a new friend, and he doesn't take no for an answer. His target, a designer, rejects him and a series of bad consequences follows.

Director: Ben Stiller

Additional Cast: Matthew Broderick, Leslie Mann, Jack Black,
    George Segal, Dane Baker, Ben Stiller

Ace Ventura: When Nature Calls (1995)

Plot summary: A wacky pet detective comes out of retirement to investigate the disappearance of a rare white bat, the symbol of an African tribe.

Director: Steve Oedekerk

Additional Cast: Ian McNeice, Simon Callow, Maynard Eziashi,
    Bob Gunton

Batman Forever (1995)

Plot summary: Batman must battle Two-Face and The Riddler with help of an amorous psychologist and a young circus acrobat who becomes his sidekick, Robin.

Director: Joel Schumacher

Additional Cast: Val Kilmer, Tommy Lee Jones, Nicole Kidman,
    Chris O'Donnell

Dumb and Dumber (1994)

Plot summary: The cross-country adventures of two good-hearted but incredibly stupid friends.

Director: Peter Farrelly

Additional Cast: Jeff Daniels, Lauren Holly, Mike Starr, Karen Duffy

The Mask (1994)

Plot summary: A mild-mannered bank clerk is transformed into a manic super-hero when he wears a mysterious mask.

Director: Charles Russell

Additional Cast: Peter Riegert, Peter Greene, Amy Yasbeck, Richard Jeni, Cameron Diaz

Ace Ventura: Pet Detective (1994)

Plot summary: A wacky detective specializing in animals goes in search of a stolen dolphin mascot of a football team.

Director: Tom Shadyac

Writer (Screenplay): Jim Carrey

Additional Cast: Courtney Cox, Sean Young, Tone Loc, Dan Mirino

Earth Girls Are Easy (1988)

Plot summary: A spaceship with three furry aliens lands in a California girl's swimming pool, so she makes friends with them

Director: Julien Temple

Additional Cast: Geena Davis, Jeff Goldblum, Damon Wayans, Julie Brown, Michael McKean

The Dead Pool (1988)

Plot summary: Dirty Harry Callahan must stop a sick secret contest to murder local celebrities, which includes himself as a target.

Director: Buddy Van Horn

Additional Cast: Clint Eastwood, Patricia Clarkson, Evan C. Kim, David hunt

Peggy Sue Got Married (1986)

Plot summary: When Peggy Sue faints at a high school reunion. She wakes up, and finds herself in her own past, just before she finished school.

    Director: Francis Coppola

    Additional Cast: Kathleen Turner, Nicolas Cage, Barry Miller,
        Catherine Hicks

Once Bitten (1985)

Plot summary: A vampire Countess needs to drink the blood of a virgin in order to keep her eternal beauty. It seems that all is hopeless, until she bumps into Mark Kendall.

    Director: Howard Storm

    Additional Cast: Lauren Hutton, Karen Kopins, Cleavon Little,
        Thomas Ballatore

CHAPTER 5

In His Own Words

Jim Carrey tells it like it is! He never takes himself too seriously and has the great ability to laugh at himself and at the film world to which is he still a very much sought-after actor. Some of Jim's favorite topics of discussion include, of course, his wonderfully entertaining films, his life, career, and most importantly, his family and private life.

So read on for some of the actor's most revealing and interesting quotes. As time goes on Jim Carrey's celebrity will undoubtedly increase and meet a whole new generation of admirers. You never know what's going to come out of Jim's mouth next, but you can bet he's either going to say something incredibly funny, or equally as honest.

On Life

"My focus is to forget the pain of life. Forget the pain, mock the pain, and reduce it. And laugh."

"Life opens up opportunities to you, and you either take them or you stay afraid of taking them."

"If you aren't in the moment, you are either looking forward to uncertainty, or back to pain and regret."

"Everything in my life has happened for a good reason. When I'm on the beam man the blessings just come one after another like rain."

On childhood:

"I practiced making faces in the mirror and it would drive my mother crazy. She used to scare me by saying that I was going to see the devil if I kept looking in the mirror. That fascinated me even more, of course."

On Working at the Comedy Store:

"I started to get known doing impressions and stopped doing that because I saw where it was leading and so because I did that I was able to excel to another level without being known as the comic impressionist."

On Being Funny:

"I don't feel any pressure to be funny at all. I'm funny because I want to be funny. I could sit here and be serious for an hour and you would go away and make me much funnier than I am."

"I'm a genetic imprint of my father. I would see him entertain people at my house and he'd get so animated. I'd sit back and think, 'Man, this guy is like a cartoon! That's what I want to be.'"

"There was a time when people said, 'Jim, if you keep on making faces, your face will freeze like that.' Now they just say, 'Pay him!'

On Fame:

"I enjoy fame except when I'm with my daughter. Kids stop me all the time and I don't want her to be jealous of the attention. Also, sometimes I just want to be left alone and I refuse to make rubber faces."

"I used to really want to be famous and now everyone is doing it." (On *YouTube.com*)

"You can't be a star at home."

On Growing Up With Family:

"We had problems like all families but we had a lot of love. I was extremely loved. We always felt we had each other."

"I got a lot of support from my parents. That's the one thing I always appreciated. They didn't tell me I was being stupid; they told me I was being funny."

"I think we all try to stand up for things we believe in. Truth and honesty were ingrained in me by my parents."

On His Privacy:

"I need privacy. I would think that because what I do makes a lot of people happy that I might deserve a little bit of respect in return. Instead, the papers try to drag me off my pedestal."

"I'm a hard guy to live with. I'm like a caged animal. I'm up all night walking around the living room. It's hard for me to come down from what I do."

"I tend to stay up late, not because I'm partying but because it's the only time of the day when I'm alone and don't have to be performing."

On Acting:

"I will never be satisfied until I burst into a ball of flames on-camera and the director yells, 'He got it!'"

"I want to be the greatest actor that ever lived, frankly. I'd love that. But I don't need to be. I just want to be here. That's it."

"Until *Ace Ventura*, no actor had considered talking through his ass." "I just want to be killer funny. You know kick ass piss in your pants run out of the theatre and rip you dick off and throw yourself into traffic funny!"

"I always look for characters that make the best of the circumstances they're in, not just brood about it."

On His Private Life:
"I'm really not that exciting. I'm basically a boring guy off the set."

On Lemony Snicket Being Too Scary For Younger Kids To See
(Says joking). "I don't think we can really understand the psychological ramifications of this film yet. Maybe ten years form now when this generation grows up we'll see if an abnormal number of them become serial kickers."

On the Truman Role:
This is an opportunity to show more colors. It simply came my way and I chose to do it."

"It was such a leap in my career when 'Truman Show' came along. It's always been a long process for me insofar as recognition goes, but that's OK because you appreciate it when it comes."

"What I have in common with the character in 'Truman' is this incredible need to please people. I feel like I want to take care of everyone and

I also feel this terrible guilt if I am unable to. And I have felt this way ever since all this success started."

"My life is not unlike Truman's. I can't go anywhere."

On His Career:

"It's amazing the things I've tripped into. But you can't settle for things. You've got to try doing something different. You've got to have a choice."

"My career it's like whatever, whenever, if it comes it comes, if it doesn't it doesn't. I don't sweat it."

"It's better to go after something special and risk starving to death than to surrender, if you give up your dreams, what's left?"

"I've arrived at the place if I'm not taking a career risk, I'm not happy. If I'm scared, then I know I'm being challenged."

On Love and Relationships:

"A lot of good love can happen in ten years."

"You can't help who you love."

"I'm so wrapped up in my work that it's often impossible to consider other things in my life. Maybe it's not meant for me to settle down and be married.

"Creative people don't behave very well generally. If you're looking for examples of good relationships in show business, you're gonna be depressed real fast."

On Money:

"I'm the first to admit this whole salary thing is getting out of control. In the final analysis, it's still about the work. The whole time I was filming The Cable Guy, I kept reminding myself that if a scene didn't work, the $20 million would bite me in the butt."

"I haven't been as wild with my money as somebody like me might have been. I've been very safe, very conservative with investments. I don't blow money. I don't have a ton of houses. I know things can go away. I've already had that experience."

On His Role as the Grinch:

"The Grinch is bigger than me. The Grinch is a great character, and what we ought to do is create the very best Grinch that we can."

On Working With Jennifer Aniston in Bruce Almighty:

"We worked well off each other because Jennifer is a completely different kind of person than me. I'm a person who just kind of like throws myself out there and does all kinds of wild stuff, and she's like the center of the wheel. I'm doing this all the way around her, and she's the type of person that can sit there and allow things to come to her. I seek them out and destroy them. So, you know, it's a wonderful kind of mix. She's very solid and very centered."

On His Role in The Majestic:

"This one is about manhood. I'm faced with getting older and the question of what is your legacy going to be. What are people going to say about you?"

On Tom Hanks:

"He's had an incredible career. He's really done it right."

"It's nice to finally get scripts offered to me that aren't the ones Tom Hanks wipes his butt with."

On Keeping a Positive Attitude:

"I live in a place of just go forward and do your best work and I believe in my soul and that I'm a worthwhile person, that there is something interesting to me to sit with for two hours. So, that's my faith. I have to have my faith. You don't consider when you're dealing with faith you don't consider oh my God, it might fall on its face, because that fall on its face is gonna lead, if that does happen, hopefully not, but if it does happen, it will lead to greater things."

On Working With Kate Winslet in Eternal Sunshine of the Spotless Mind:

"I get excited when the people I work with scare me. She's just scary-talented and just an amazing actress. I get excited when I'm surrounded by people who make me better and make me stay on my game and challenge me. She's wonderful to watch - unbelievable - because you sometimes don't know what she's doing when you're in a scene with her. You look at it later and she knows what's going to come off, how it's going to look. It's beautiful."

On the Erasing-Memory Theme of Eternal Sunshine of the Spotless Mind:

"I loved the idea that the memories went in reverse. There were so many things that made it different than your normal losing-your-memory movie. I love the clunky, sci-fi aspect of this movie. It doesn't take it over; it's just a function within it. It's interesting."

On Being an Accomplished Actor:

"I ran into a lot of criticism ... 'Be the comedian. Like why is he trying to do that? They're all trying to do that,' kind of thing. And, I believe in that side of myself, absolutely. So, I'm willing to lose everything to express that side of myself. I'm willing to give it all up."

"It's better to go after something special and risk starving to death than to surrender, if you give up your dreams, what's left?"

On Battling Depression:

"I was on Prozac for a long time. It may have helped me out of a jam for a little bit, but people stay on it forever. I had to get off at a certain point because I realized that, you know, everything's just okay."

"There are peaks, there are valleys. But they're all kind of carved and smoothed out, and it feels like a low level of despair you live in. Where you're not getting any answers, but you're living okay. And you can smile at the office. You know? But it's a low level of despair. You know?"

"I don't think anybody is interesting until they've had the shit kicked out of them. The pain is there for a reason. A lot of times when I was in those depressions, I also had the thing going through my head that this is what I've asked for."

On Desperation:

"People need motivation to do anything. I don't think human beings learn anything without desperation. Desperation is a necessary ingredient to learning anything, or creating anything. Period. If you ain't desperate at some point, you ain't interesting."

On Comedy Verses Dramatic Roles:

"I like being creative, period. I think it is important to never overlook our talents."

On God and Faith:

"I don't think you can know God unless you're passionate about him so you're either screaming at him, enraptured with the idea of being around him or feeling him in your life."

"I've prayed to God that I would have depth as an artist and have things to say. I've said, No matter what, keep me sane but give me what I need."

"If I'm alright myself, if I'm alright with God and doing the right things with my life - it's incredible. The monsoon of blessings that come to me. I've been so lucky. I've had so many miracles in my life that it's incredible."

On Playing Ebeneezer Scrooge:

"Ebeneezer is such a great thing for me, because again, I get to play all kinds of different roles. in the film. And first of all, the process is so fascinating. You're literally in an empty warehouse with cameras around you. And you have – maybe a frame of a fireplace, or something like that. And then you rehearse, and they go, 'Can we take this away?' you're sitting on a chair. And you have to create the entire world in your head."

CHAPTER 6

What Others Say About Jim Carrey

What's it like to work with Jim Carrey? You can bet it's not boring! Here's what some famous and behind the scenes friends and associates say about their unique and interesting experiences working with the beloved actor.

"There's something alien about Jim Carrey. He's like Charlie Chaplin or Buster Keaton. If Jim Carrey had been around in the 1920s, he would have been a silent star. He's easy going, but pretty occupied."— Peter Weir

"Jim's never really come out and said this, but I don't think he likes the idea that it's plastered everywhere what he's earning. I don't think he wants it to overshadow the work itself."— Nicolas Cage

"Jim did stuff that tapped into some weird energy that's inside of him. I don't know where it comes from. All I can say is I'm glad he has an outlet for it."— Ben Stiller, (*The Cable Guy*)

"Working with him is like visiting an insane asylum."— Cameron Diaz (*The Mask*)

"When I saw him in *Dumb & Dumber* I believed that it was a miracle: he's my son! I think Jim Carrey is brilliant." — Jerry Lewis

"The coolest person I've ever worked with is Jim Carrey. Jim is great. I learned a lot from him. You see him in films and you think he's just zany and off the wall. You'd think the director yells, 'Action!' and he just does whatever and hopes the camera captures something remotely funny."— Anthony Anderson (Actor)

"He isn't a megalomaniac like they say, he's a good boy."— Clint Eastwood

"Every time Jim Carrey was on, I was mad because it wasn't me. He's ten times funnier!'— David Spade

"*Ace Ventura* was like a slice of ginger on the palate of America. It taught people you can't know what to expect from Jim."—Tom Shadyac

"Jim is really good actor. Best of all, you keep wondering, 'What is this guy going to do?' But I think he is very honest. There's a certain innocence and vulnerability."— Ed Harris

"Working with Jim is kind of like spending your life driving on a highway and suddenly you've entered the Indy 500. When he kicks into overdrive, you just go with him. Jim will walk into a room and take a five-foot fall flat on his back, and if he gets a laugh from the crew, he'll do it again. And if not, he'll come in and make it an eight-foot fall." — Jeff Daniels (*Dumb and Dumber*)

"He's a great guy. We have such a good relationship and you can't act chemistry. You can't make that happen, so I really just hoped to God that we were going to get on well, and thankfully we didn't hate each other. So, it was just great. Yes, he's kind of goofy and silly and pulls crazy faces. My God, he is a master impersonator."— Kate Winslet (*Eternal Sunshine of the Spotless Mind*)

"Jim Carrey keeps wanting to do drama. I say shut up and just do comedy, make $100 million and relax. Actors always want to be the thing they are not."— James Wood

"Jim is really good actor. Best of all, you keep wondering, 'What is this guy going to do?' But I think he is very honest. There's a certain innocence and vulnerability."—Ed Harris (*The Truman Show*)

"I was so shocked by his lack of narcissism. Sometimes when I was acting with him, his eyes would and other times his eyes would glaze, so I wasn't sure what I was getting, because I was giving him a lot of psychic energy."—Courtney Love *(Man on the Moon)*

"Jim is extremely sexy. His face, his body, his height. He is kind of lanky and loose and relaxed. He's got a handsome, straightforward, Midwestern look." —Swoosie Kurtz

"The sexiest thing about Jim Carrey is his humor. Let's face it, every woman likes to be made to laugh."—Amanda Donohoe *(Liar Liar)*

"Jim is like one of those huge organs in an old church with thousands of pedals and pip. He can play Jimmy Stewart in *It's A Wonderful Life* or he can play the devil or he can play *Dumb & Dumber*, Lauren and Hardy, or the Marx Brothers." — Joel Schumacher

"He's a very arts and craftsy kind of guy. He knit me a sweater. It's pink." — Noah Emmerich (*The Truman Show*)

"The first time I met him, I looked at him and thought, 'God, he looks like Cary Grant.' You don't think of that when you think of Jim Carrey, but when you can just look at him, he's this big, handsome, strapping man." —Laura Linney (*The Truman Show*)

"Jim's a great looking guy, he can do the leading man. He's got a unique package there — someone who is really good looking and funny. The possibilities are endless."—Richard Belzer

"When you know that it's Jim, first of all you can write thinking about him. And I've worked with him before so that's always fun, and you also know that he will execute it better than you wrote it. He's also going to have a lot of ideas of his own so it becomes a real collaboration with him."— Judd Apatow (Writer for *Fun With Dick and Jane*)

"Jim is amazing. He is an artist of the highest order. While Kaufman was sometimes a blow for surrealism, Jim was always a gentleman and always generous." — Lorne Michaels

"He's so funny and I've seen all of his films and I have a very similar wacky sense of humor, so I expected him to be a lot wackier when I met him. He's just a real sweet, as normal as Jim Carrey can be since he's a big movie star. But he's just a real nice normal guy and has a kind heart and I knew from the first day of filming that we were on our journey to tell something really beautiful, because we both had to be so vulnerable and open up our hearts. It was magical." — Laurie Holden (*The Majestic*)

"He's heavily sedated and he's trying to stick-shift the gurney and drive it making 'brrrmm-brrmm' sounds with his mouth." Wayne Flemming (*Fun With Dick and Jane*) on Jim's gall bladder surgery in 1994.

"Jim Carrey is always surprising people. So now I hear that he takes a little bit of a dramatic turn so I think he's extremely versatile and some-times an actor just needs the opportunity to show the other side of himself."— Ving Rhames

"Every time I hear his name, I laugh."—KT Rowe (*The Number 23*)

CHAPTER 7

Jim Carrey Trivia –
INCLUDING THE ULTIMATE QUIZ

So, you think you know everything there is to know about Jim Carrey from his films and comedy performances to television appearances and his much guarded personal life. That's impressive! Well, we think we can still stump you. If you answer 80 percent of these questions correctly you will win our private Rubber Face Award. And, no peeking throughout this book for the answers!

QUESTIONS

1. In which film did Jim Carrey play a character named Lloyd Christmas?

2. Jim Carrey was actually the second choice to play the Riddler in *Batman Forever*. Who was the first?

3. At age 16, Jim dropped out of high school to work with his family. What job did the Carrey family take on?

4. How many times has Carrey been nominated for an Academy Award?

5.　What country was Jim Carrey born?

6.　TRUE OR FALSE: *The Cable Guy* was nominated for a Golden Globe award.

7.　TRUE OR FALSE:　By mid-2000 Jim was being paid $20 million per film.

8.　What was the name of the very short-lived TV show Jim had early in his career?

9.　Jim portrayed what famous green character in a popular children's movie?

10.　What is Jim's middle name?

11.　What was the name of the TV show that Jim co-starred in portraying a character named "Fire Marshal Bill"?

12.　What year was Jim born?

13.　What is the occupation of Jim's character in *Me, Myself, and Irene*?

14.　TRUE OR FALSE:　In *Liar Liar*, Jim plays an FBI agent.

15.　What is Jim's character doing in the beginning of *Ace Ventura: When Nature Calls*?

16.　What famous villain did Jim portray in the film *Batman Forever*?

17.　What actor portrays Jim's co-star in the movie *Dumb and Dumber*?

18.　In *The Truman Show*, what was Truman's full name?

19.　What famous actress was Jim dating in 2000?

20.　In *Man on the Moon*, Jim Carrey portrayed what famous comedian?

21.　After he became famous for outrageous comedy films, Jim turned the tables and took on the first of serious roles.　Name that film.

22. Name the character he played in that film.

23. In the made for TV movie, *Copper Mountain*, name the character Jim played.

24. Before he became famous, Jim wrote himself a post-dated check for how much?

25. What was the *Mask* character originally based on?

26. In *Batman Forever*, Jim portrays the Riddler. What is the Riddler's real name?

27. Name the two songs he sang in that film?

28. TRUE OR FALSE: Jim loves to rent DVD movies and watch them at home.

29. Jim played the best friend of his real-life pal Nicolas Cage in what film?

30. In 1999, Jim performed two songs with a rock band at a private concert he arranged. What was the name of the band?

31. Jim's catch phrase, "All righty then," appeared in what film?

32. At 17, Jim made his comedic debut at this club.

33. Name the short-lived NBC 1984 sit-com Jim had starred in.

34. In 1983, Jim made his debut in what film?

35. What are Jim's parents' names?

36. How tall is Jim?

37. In the Presidential Reunion (video short), what U.S. president did Jim portray?

38. What blonde actress co-starred with Jim in *The Mask*?

39. What is the name of the character Jim plays in *The Majestic*?

40. How old was Jim when his family moved to Toronto?

41. Jim married Lauren Holly in what year and what year did they divorce?

42. In *Ace Ventura*, what animal does Jim's character fear the most?

43. In *The Truman Show,* how does Jim's character escape his artificial world?

44. What actor shared the screen with Jim in *Ace Ventura: Pet Detective?*

45. Name the actor who played Jim's partner in crime in *Batman Forever.*

46. TRUE OR FALSE: Jim has a real chipped front tooth which he had the tooth crown removed for his role in *Dumb and Dumber.*

47. What year did Jim receive U.S. citizenship?

48. Jim received the Canada's Walk of Fame star in what year?

49. What did Jim change the name of his current production company to?

50. Name the two Jim Carrey films that had the highest US Box Office sales.

ANSWERS

1. *Dumb and Dumber*
2. Robin Williams
3. Maintenance workers in a tire factory
4. Never
5. Canada
6. False
7. True
8. *The Duck Factory*
9. The Grinch
10. Eugene
11. *In Living Color*
12. 1962
13. Highway Patrol Officer
14. False
15. Rescuing a raccoon
16. The Riddler
17. Jeff Daniels
18. Truman Burbank
19. Renee Zellweger
20. Andy Kaufman
21. *The Cable Guy*
22. Chip Douglas
23. Bob
24. 10 Million
25. Dark Horse comic book
26. Edward Nygma
27. "Come Together" and "Hey You"
28. True
29. *Peggy Sue Got Married*
30. Phish
31. *Ace Ventura, Pet Detective*
32. Yuk Yuk Club
33. *Ronald Reagan*
34. *All in Good Taste*
35. Percy and Kathleen
36. 6'2"
37. Andy Kaufman
38. Cameron Diaz
39. Pete Appleton/Luke Trimble
40. 8
41. 1996 and 1997
42. A Bat
43. By walking through a door
44. Tone-Loc
45. Tommy Lee Jones
46. True
47. October 7, 2004
48. 1998
49. JC 23 Entertainment
50. *How The Grinch Stole Christmas* ($260,044.825 and *Bruce Almighty* ($242, 829.261)

For this book, hundreds of Jim Carrey fans were polled via the Internet to see what projections they had for the multi-talented actor. The following Top Five suggestions came up the most and are listed in order of popularity.

In addition to this list, and this is a given, many fans would really like to own a complete collection of all Jim Carrey films to date in one big box collection on DVD.

Top Five Projections

1. For Jim to continue making more movies (both comedy and drama).

2. For Jim to finally win an Oscar (and he certainly deserves it!).

3. For Jim to write an entire film script and star in the film.

4. For Jim to record an album of his favorite songs (and to write his own song as well).

5. For Jim to write his autobiography or memoirs (including a glimpse into his private life).

CHAPTER 8

Collecting Carrey

Though Jim Carrey's career has only spanned over two decades, it keeps getting stronger with each introduction to a new generation of fans. Collecting Jim Carrey memorabilia has never been so rewarding as well as profitable— for fans of all ages.

There are literally hundreds of items to collect—mostly official movie memorabilia and props that include signed and unsigned movie posters, scripts, calendars, photos, candles, coffee mugs and magnets as well as more rare and hard to find pieces like clothing in films worn by Jim.

What does the serious Jim Carrey fan search for in memorabilia? For starters, usually something they don't have. If you enjoy collecting signed 8 x10" movie photos, most likely would want one from every film. Other fans that collect movie posters would do the same.

Some of the even more serious fans may take it a step further and video record all of his television appearances—mostly interviews to promote whatever new movie is out at the moment. In fact, many of our survey respondents said they were in the process transferring all the videotaped television appearances to DVD. Now that's dedication!

A typical collector may be happy with just having their Jim Carrey DVD movie collection completely up to date. Some were doing the same with their articles collection. Even a few ardent female fans claimed to be personalizing their Jim Carrey articles and photo collections with today's latest scrap booking materials.

"Jim Carrey fans are loyal and enthusiastic in their collecting needs," said Miles, a collector in Europe. "I've made many friends over the years. I've seen many different levels of collecting. Most Jim Carrey fans go for the DVDs and movie posters, especially if an American fan is looking for the foreign movie posters."

Our survey has shown there are various levels of Jim Carrey fandom, and a select few obsessive collectors search for movie props and personal clothing. You can own an item of Jim Carrey apparel or movie prop simply by visiting eBay.com and searching under categories: Entertainment Memorabilia, Movie Memorabilia, and Movie Props.

Of course, there are other popular online sources to like Star Wares Collectibles (also on eBay), which is located in Agoura, California. Owners Marica Tysseling and her brother John are lifelong film and television fans who offer thousands of personal celebrity items, wardrobe and movie props at very reasonable prices. Up to fifty percent of the profits go to deserving and important charities such as Elizabeth Taylor Aids Foundation, Last Chance For Animals, Big Sisters Of Los Angeles, Heal the Bay, and Starlight Foundation, to name a few.

Most of the Jim Carrey items come directly from various movie studios, production companies or from the actor himself. "Over the years we have sold lots of Jim Carrey clothing and movie props," offered a store representative. "Mostly from *Ace Ventura* to *Bruce Almighty*. Fans call or email us, usually looking for something familiar from one of his movies."

With more than 17 years in the business, StarWares has become a recognized leader of collecting and selling of authentic Hollywood merchandise. Thousands of delighted and satisfied fans from around the world not only revel in the thought of owning a piece of Hollywood history, but also know that their purchases help contribute to worthy causes and charities.

"We maintain an excellent reputation in the industry for authenticity and personal customer service," added the salesperson. "If a customer is looking for a special Jim Carrey item that we don't have, we will use our vast resources and try to locate it for them."

Celebrity clothing and personal items collecting through internet auctions like eBay and Yahoo have become increasing popular over the years and quite profitable to boot. The best advice we can offer a seasoned Carrey memorabilia collector — who knows the value of autographed items, but has no clue about the significance of owning a movie prop or costume worn by Carrey like a Grinch or Count Oalf outfit — is that it's more important to purchase pieces that can be authenticated or come with a money back guarantee.

Start out simply and be careful of the authentication of any item. Always ask the seller to see a verifiable copy of the C.O.A prior to the close of the auction.

Whether you are novice or a 20-year collector, it is wise to never put a financial strain on your budget. Collecting memorabilia on Jim Carrey should be a fun and rewarding experience where you can meet other like-minded people along the way. If you can't buy collectible piece of Carrey memorabilia you want the first time around, you will most likely have a second chance thanks to the wonderful services of eBay.

Top Five Most Collectible Jim Carrey Items

Our book survey polled fans on their Top Five favorite Carrey collectibles. In order of popularity:

1. Self-made DVD and video tapes of television appearances (mostly interviews and entertainment news shows)

2. Autographed photographs or movie posters

3. Promotional photographs or still from movies

4.   Self-made article scrapbooks and/or photo albums

5.   Books (biographies or film books)

Jim Carrey Memorabilia Sold On eBay, and How Much It Went For...

Besides television and film memorabilia shows, eBay has proved to be the best source for satisfying your Jim Carrey collecting needs. In no particular, order these collectibles ranked as the most popular.

One-of-a-kind Hollywood movie props— the latex The Riddler eye mask from *Batman Forever*.... $250.00

From *Fun With Dick and Jane*—The black and gray water pistol held by Jim's Dick Harper character... $269.00

Jim Carrey hand signed film scripts: *The Mask; Dumb and Dumber; Ace Ventura: Pet Detective* and *Liar Liar*... $25.00 - $55.00

Original 27 x 40" (*Me, Myself and Irene; The Majestic; Fun With Dick and Jane; Eternal Sunshine of the Spotless Mind; Bruce Almighty; The Truman Show* and *Lemony Snicket: A Series of Unfortunate Events*)... $9.99 - $16.95

Ace Ventura: When Nature Calls — 14 inch promotional necklace ... $19.95

Jim Carrey hand-signed promotional black and white 8 x 10" movie stills from *Ace Ventura* (One and Two); *The Mask; The Truman Show;, Me, Myself and Irene; Batman Forever* and *Bruce Almighty*... $14.95 - $19.95

Jim Carrey hand-signed promotional black and white 11 x

14" movie stills from *Me, Myself and Irene; Liar Liar; Dumb and Dumber; The Cable Guy* and *Bruce Almighty* ... $16.95 - $22.95

One-of-a-kind *The Mask* continuity Polaroids of Jim Carrey... $60.00

Liar Liar promotional coffee mug ... $15.95

Rare child-size *The Mask* costume ... $25.00

Rare adult-size *The Mask* costume ... $45.00

Jim Carrey non-movie signed 8 x10" color photograph with matted frame ... $16.95 - $22.95

Jim Carrey movie press kits (early films to present) ... $12.95 -$25.00

Bruce Almighty lobby card ... $13.50 - $15.50

Ace Ventura: When Nature Calls movie prop: The Native Shield ... $79.50

Talking Riddler Doll from *Batman Forever* ... $25.00

Investment Pieces – Jim Carrey-Worn Movie Costumes

Original Jim Carrey Costume from *How The Grinch Stole Christmas* (Santa Claus costume) ... $14,000

Original Jim Carrey Riddler Green Bowler Hat from *Batman Forever* ...$4,000

Original On-Screen Used Who Mail (2) Envelopes From Whoville Post Office ...$95.00

Original Jim Carrey Riddler "Question Mark" Costume
From *Batman Forever* ... $10,000

Top Five Wish List of Jim Carrey Collectibles Fans Want To Own

Serious collecting fans were asked to name the top five Jim Carrey items they would like to own. We were surprised at the findings. Here they are the results in order of popularity.

1. Any of the more familiar and outlandish clothing and hats Jim wore in films: *The Mask; Batman Forever; How The Grinch Stole Christmas; Lemony Snicket's a Series of Unfortunate Events* and *Ace Ventura* (one and two).

2. The Hawaiian signature shirt Jim wore in *Ace Ventura* or the familiar flannel shirt in *Bruce Almighty*.

3. Any familiar prop from his movies.

4. His real phone or email address! (We swear!)

5. A personal handwritten letter or note from Jim acknowledging that they are his biggest fan ever.

Part 2

CHAPTER 9

The Carreyholics Society

For more than two decades, Jim Carrey has earned legions of loyal fans. He has evolved from funny man to serious actor in some of the most memorable and lucrative films of his career. There is no question that Jim Carrey will remain one of the most beloved actors of the 21st century. He has been making people both chuckle and roar with laughter since he was a kid back in Canada. From his one-man shows in the family basement and standup comedy in Los Angeles nightclubs to the hit TV show *In Living Color* and finally to a succession of major big screen films, Jim Carrey was destined to be one of Hollywood's biggest stars.

This book's survey embodied many important aspects of the popular actor's allure, beginning with a question on how they became a fan in the first place. The number one response was the inevitable: Jim Carrey's film roles and television appearances (particularly as a cast member of *In Living Color*). Even Jim Carrey himself will tell you he doesn't quite understand why so many people love and revere him, but at the same time he is so grateful for all the attention.

Perhaps what people admire most about Jim Carrey, aside from his ability to make people laugh with his memorable films, is his incredible diverse acting talent. In addition to being one of Hollywood's most bankable comedians, Jim Carrey has also proved himself to be a critically acclaimed dramatic actor.

Jim can certainly be funny without being over the top. Movies like *Liar Liar, Bruce Almighty* and *Fun with Dick and Jane* show that he has the talent and ability to seamlessly integrate humor and still come across as believable to the viewer. It's easy to appreciate Jim for his inane sense of humor— the silly faces he makes in all his movies, but to truly appreciate Jim Carrey the dramatic actor you have to watch *Eternal Sunshine of the Spotless Mind* and forget (no pun intended!) that he has the lead role. Some would say his seemingly effortless performance is uncanny.

"What an amazing performance Jim Carrey gave in *Eternal Sunshine*," noted Robert F. of Brooklyn, New York. "You get so immersed in the story and the intense emotions and what's happening in the movie, that you really start to feel for his character. The film is such a departure from his earlier funnier ones. Even his acting in *Truman* is nowhere what he's achieved in *Eternal Sunshine*."

"Jim Carrey is an outstanding actor in a serious role," offered a Canadian fan. "If he would just stick with these kind of roles, he may finally win an Oscar. He certainly deserves it. I remember seeing him play an alcoholic teen in *Doing Time on Maple Drive*. He had it even back then. He didn't have to be funny to prove he can act."

Since the early 90s, Jim Carrey has attained a solid circle of faithful fans ranging from as young as age five to eighty-five. With each new film or performing project, Jim Carrey always seems to win over more converts — and his longtime loyal followers remain eternally connected to him, perhaps stronger than ever since the 2004 release of *Eternal Sunshine of the Spotless Mind*.

If we were able to create a formula for success, Jim Carrey's career would make an intriguing model. From stand up comedy and celebrity impressions to television and films, this gifted actor is undoubtedly one of the chosen few from a small and elite group of modern day film icons.

"I have been a loyal fan since the *In Living Color* days," said Nancy, a *Jim Carrey Online* member. "Jim has an amazing amount of talent, and he's never afraid to take risks. He's very versatile. I laugh out loud at some of his roles, and cry my eyes out at other ones. You're never sure what he's going to do next, and that makes him so exciting to watch. I was originally more of a fan of his comedic roles, but as he has developed more as an actor, I tend to prefer his dramatic roles. Overall, he is simply awesome!"

"You can't deny that Jim Carrey is one of the best comedians in the world. I've been a fan since day one," Mark B. from Ontario, Canada writes. "I remember seeing him when he did impressions of famous people like Jack Nicholson and Clint Eastwood. He's more than just a funny guy— he's a naturally funny guy."

Salvatore from Milan, Italy agreed, "I am one of Jim Carrey's greatest fans. To me, he is one of the funniest actors in the world. I admire him for his ability to make people laugh and his honesty and dedication to his profession."

Chris from Belgium said, "Every time there is a new Jim Carrey movie coming out, I get really excited. I never get tired of watching him because he always comes up with something new. Jim Carrey knows how to really keep it entertaining and interesting for his fans."

Dan from Canada concurred, "Jim is such a respectful man. He doesn't do movies for the money. He does it because they are different or he has something to prove. He is exceptional in both comedy and drama roles. Jim has this 'underdog' aura about him. He has something to prove and I want to see him prove those people wrong that do not believe in him. He is by no means a one-dimensional actor."

No argument here. There are those few who feel the actor has made an unbelievable significant difference in their lives. As Daniel J. attested: "Jim Carrey inspired me in a way I will never forget. I was five years old when I first saw *The Mask*. I loved it so much. I have seen every Jim Carrey movie since then and never miss a talk show appearance. I can't help but admire him. In school I used to act like him. He was always sort of a hero to me. I am now trying to break into acting. If I make it, I will thank Jim Carrey for being my biggest influence."

Survey respondents also sensed that Jim possesses qualities that they would possibly look for in a special friend: humor, honesty, loyalty, generosity, and genuine concern for one's fellow man (like his YouTube plea to release Aung San Suu Kyi). When describing what makes Jim Carrey so unique to so many, respondents pointed out how he has influenced or changed their lives on a deeply personal level.

"Jim Carrey is a big inspiration to me," said Laura, another big Canadian fan. "My admiration of Jim comes from knowing his dream of success came true because he never stopped believing in himself. Real life gets nasty sometimes and Jim's success helps me keep my dream alive."

Fans were asked if they preferred the actor in comedy or drama roles. Interestingly enough, many reported they enjoyed Carrey's on-screen performances more in comedy rather than drama. "He belongs doing comedy. That's what he does best," said a loyal fan from Sweden. "He makes me laugh. He makes the world laugh and we need more funny people like Jim Carrey."

A fan in India added, "The reason why I prefer Jim Carrey in comedy is because anyone can make people cry, but to make people laugh is much tougher, and Jim Carrey makes it look easy."

Then there were those fans that loved both his work in comedy and drama and simply couldn't decide. "Jim is the best actor out there. I love everything he does. I like both his comedy and drama roles. I can't choose," acknowledged Marcella, a fan from Italy. "I think most people think he's better at the funny stuff because that's what he's known more for, but he is equally entertaining in his serious roles as well. If you say you are a true fan of Jim Carrey, then you should support his choices of the movies he wants to make."

Judging by the consensus, Jim doesn't seem to disappoint his legion of fans with his film performances (though some noted movie critics beg to differ). Everyone has a favorite and least favorite Jim Carrey film. The survey asked what was the absolute all-time favorite film. This, you can imagine, brought on even more agonizing over the answers!

Anthony, from Teaneck, New Jersey, finds the actor a "true blessing" especially when he's in high form. "For me, Jim Carrey is at his absolutely best when he portrays villains like The Riddler, The Grinch and even Count Olaf to a degree. I would have to say my favorite film is *The Grinch* one. He showed his most creative work ever."

"*Dumb and Dumber* is funnier than *Liar Liar*," offered Staci from Cleveland, Ohio. "*Dumber* is the one I put into the DVD player when I need some cheering up. *Bruce Almighty* would have to be third. I think Jim does his best work when he is being funny."

"Jim Carrey is the funniest guy in the world! He knows how to make people laugh before he even opens his mouth," William, a lifelong admirer, added. "Remember he's the funny actor who got his start in slapstick comedy shows like *In Living Color*. Jim Carrey has gone beyond being a household name, not just because he is known for being funny, but also because he is such a diverse actor. His best movies shouldn't have to be the gut-bustin' hilarious ones like the *Ace Venturas, Dumber, Liar Liar,* or *Bruce Almighty*. He is every bit as amazing in films like *Eternal Sunshine, The Truman Show* or *The Majestic*. I personally never get tired of watching my DVDs of any of his films, especially *The Truman Show* or *Fun With Dick and Jane*."

Some fans that responded were quick to mention Carrey's very earliest of serious performances in the made for Canadian television film like *Doing Time On Maple Drive*. Tim from Quebec, Canada, offered: "Jim was very young when he did *Doing Time on Maple Drive*. I think that was his first serious role and he was really good. He was so convincing as a teenage alcoholic. I remember hearing back then what a big break it was for him. You know, we Canadians are very proud of Jim Carrey's success."

Who doesn't admire an actor that can be both the funny *and* romantic lead at the same time? With the ease of a pro, Carrey makes you laugh in one film and then makes you cry in another. Overall, hundreds of fans from around the world all seem to agree that it's a given that Carrey is "a great actor" when it comes to comedy roles. But there are those few who don't give him a "fair shot" in other types of roles because humor is *expected*. "Just because he has been doing comedy for such a long time— well most of his career, doesn't mean people can't see him in another light," summed up another longtime fan. "I can enjoy seeing *The Majestic* and *The Truman Show* just as much as I love *The Number 23*. Films like *The Number 23* or *Eternal Sunshine of the Spotless Mind* are not exactly how we are used to seeing Jim Carrey, but that's what makes him so different and more endearing than the rest of the actors out there."

Of course, the survey wouldn't be complete without asking some of the most adamant Jim Carrey fans worldwide to choose their least favorite film or films. This included the minor roles as well. These choices were unanimous straight across the board: *Copper Mountain*, *Rubber Face* and *All In Good Taste*. These films were made early in his career and not considered by the actor or his fans to be true Jim Carrey films.

As for sequels (other than *Ace Ventura: When Nature Calls*), what do fans hope to see their favorite actor star in the future? *The Cable Guy* and *Lemony Snicket's Series of Unfortunate Events* came up the most. *Bruce Almighty* came in third. Jim has stated that he isn't big on sequels and it would have to be something that he really wants to do.

"Jim rocked in *The Cable Guy* and in *Lemony Snicket*—it would be cool if there were sequels to these two films," noted one fan. "Though *Lemony Snicket* is already a series, the film simply didn't seem complete to me. I think a lot of people felt that way. As for *Ace Ventura*, don't see why he couldn't do another one. More than 10 years have passed. That would be interesting. If Bruce Willis could do so many *Die Hard* movies, why can't Jim Carrey do a third *Ace Ventura*. I would go see it."

"I'm glad he didn't do the horrible *Son of The Mask* film or even that absolutely disgraceful *Dumb and Dumberer*," another fan stated.

When asked what fans expect to see from the actor in the future, the answers were all pretty much all in unison: "For Jim to make more great movies!" As an actor, Jim is no less than a consummate professional giving his all to fans. It's no wonder why we have seen many of his films dozens of times and enjoy sharing memories and favorite scenes.

"I don't know what I would do if there were no more Jim Carrey movies made," concluded Lisa W., from Rowlett, Texas. "I hope Jim Carrey is as happy as he makes us fans when we see his movies and I hope he continues doing what he does best— making movies that entertain us."

LAURA LAING FROM CANADA:

AN EARLY ENCOUNTER WITH JIM CARREY

I have a few Jim Carrey stories to tell.

Back in 1976, Jim and his family lived in Burlington, ON, kitty-corner from my family in a townhouse complex. The first time I 'noticed' Jim was in my grade nine-art class at Aldershot High School. I can remember watching him draw a sketch of John Wayne, and saying, 'I'm going shade you in pilgrim', in the most amazing John Wayne vocal impersonation.

The next time I saw Jim was four years later. The grade 12 English teacher from Aldershot H.S. met Jim while he was performing at Yuk Yuk's in Toronto. He made arrangements to have Jim come back and perform for the entire school. We had a friendly chat prior to his performance.

A few months later I attended a performance at Yuk Yuk's with another friend. During his performance at that time, Jim would do an improv bit where he asked for the audience to shout out ideas. We shouted out "Aldershot High School" Jim's reaction was priceless. He spun around, ran off the stage down to where we were seated, shoved his face in ours, then ran back up on stage pointing at us, and exclaimed, 'I know those people!' He proceeded to impersonate the school principal while singing the school song. He had the crowd in stitches. We met backstage after the show and chatted for a bit.

During the next couple of years I went to see Jim a few times at a club called Cafe in the Park in Toronto. During that time I was attending Sheridan College in Oakville, studying Classical Animation. After one of his performance he came and joined myself and some of my fellow animation students. The conversation was quite amazing since it was right at the time that Jim was working out plans for *The Duck Factory*. He asked me to attend a party with him after the show that night, unfortunately I had to decline, but I did get a good night kiss, along with some photos of the two of us together.

Ten years later I saw Jim again when he was in Toronto doing a breakfast show with a local radio station promoting *the Peoples' Comedy Festival*. There was about a 20 minute a break in-between the two segments of the radio show, which gave us an opportunity to sit-down and do some reminiscing and takes a few photos. That was the last opportunity I had to speak with Jim, as they say, the rest is history.

Fans Pick Top Five Films

This was not an easy poll to acquire. Hundreds of fans were asked what they considered to be their favorite and least favorite of all major Jim Carrey films. You may be as surprised as we were...

Top 5 Favorite Jim Carrey Films

1. *Ace Ventura: Pet Detective*

2. *The Mask*

3. *The Truman Show*

4. *Man on the Moon*

5. *Eternal Sunshine of the Spotless Mind*

Top 5 Least Favorite Jim Carrey Films

1. *Batman Forever*

2. *Earth Girls Are Easy*

3. *The Cable Guy*

4. *The Majestic*

5. *The Number 23*

Top Five Jim Carrey Movie Sequels

1. *Ace Ventura 3*

2. *The Mask 3*

3. *Dumb and Dumber 3*

4. *The Cable Guy*

5. *Lemony Snicket: A Series of Unfortunate Events*

Jim Carrey Online

Perhaps the Number One best website for Jim Carrey fans is *Jim Carrey Online*. This site was created in 1996 by a German fan, Lars Brauer. Like millions of other film goers, he was "stunned" by Jim Carrey's performance in *Ace Ventura: Pet Detective*. More than a decade later, the site is still going strong and better than ever under the guidance of editor-in-chief, Tommy Pihl.

In 2006, Brauer wrote on the award-winning website: "Ten years have passed so quickly and so many things have changed, but *JCO* is still here and of course up to date, unlike so many other sites on the internet. So let's just hope JCO will be there for another 10 years!" No doubt the over-six-million-hits-a-year website and inexhaustible resource tool for Jim Carrey fans will be around much longer than just a mere decade more.

Pre-Video Sharing Fame

Thanks to the invention of popular video sharing sites like YouTube, MySpace, Google and others, Jim Carrey is perhaps relieved and very grateful he found fame, some 15 years earlier. "YouTube is everywhere," Carrey told a reporter. "There's a plumber right now who's mining a fortune from his butt crack I'm sure."

Our book survey asked fans to name their Top 10 Jim Carrey video spots on *YouTube.com*. You may be surprised: we were! In order of popularity:

1.   CSI: David Caruso Style on *David Letterman Late Show*

2.   *The Number 23* Enigma

3.   *In Living Color*: Fire Marshall Bill (United Nations Space Station skit)

4. *In Living Color*: Karate Instructor (complete self-defense for women skit)

5. Speaking on Steven Spielberg at the American Film Institute Awards.

6. Jim Carrey is Rocky Balboa (*Rocky VI* skit on Grace Jones comedy skit parody)

7. Celebrity imitations (from Polish television special)

8. Speaking on Meryl Streep at the American Film Institute Awards.

9. *Bruce Almighty* Bloopers

10. *Bruce Almighty:* Anchorman in trouble

CHAPTER 10

Fan Favorite Jim Carrey
Movie One-Liners And Quotes

Jim Carrey has attained a wide range of fans ranging from ages five to eighty-five, and everyone has favorite scene or line from one of his movies. Hundreds of fans were polled and asked to pick their five favorite movie quotes and it was no easy feat by any means. What follows are the results.

Of course we expected the usual catch phrases from the comedy flicks, but didn't anticipate such a response for Carrey's more serious roles. Here are the majority of results,which are not in order of popularity. How many do *you* recognize straight away?

"Allrighty then!"

"It's the cable guy."

"What did you call me?"

"Riddle me this, riddle me that, who's afraid of the big black bat?"

"You know what the trouble about real life is? There's no danger music."

"How do you make somebody love you without affecting free will?

"You don't know the real me."

"I can be your best friend or your worst enemy."

"The fact that my client has been ridden more than Seattle Slew is irrelevant."

"You have zero messages. That's odd, better check the outgoing. If you utter so much as one syllable, I'll hunt you down and gut you like a fish!"

"Smokin'!"

"Of course time is just a counting system... numbers with meanings attached to them."

"Time is a monster that cannot be reasoned with. It responds like a snail to our impatience, then it races like a gazelle when you can't catch a breath."

"I don't wanna be a vampire, I'm a day person!"

"I just wanna hang out...No big deal!"

"For I will be as a fly on the wall — a grain of salt in the ocean. I will move amongst them like a transparent... thing."

"And that's the way the cookie crumbles!"

"Somebody help me, I'm being spontaneous."

"I can't stand the constant nagging. I'm leaving you, Jerry. I'm leaving you - and I'm taking the monkey with me."

"I sped. I followed too closely. I ran a stop sign. I almost hit a Chevy. I sped some more. I failed to yield at a crosswalk. I changed lanes at the intersection. I changed lanes without signaling while running a red light and speeding."

"I come from Caspiar. It is a very small island in the Caspian Sea...it sunk."

"Am I just eating because I'm bored?"

"Smite me, oh mighty Smiter."

"Valentine's Day is a holiday invented by greeting card companies to make people feel like crap."

"Hold me closer Ed, it's getting dark. Tell Auntie Em to let Old Yeller out."

Your request is not unlike your lower intestine: stinky and loaded with danger."

"A week ago, the only thing I thought was out of the ordinary was that it was my birthday."

"Our love is like a red, red rose... and I am a little thorny."

"I'm as light as a feather! Merry as a schoolboy!"

"Look Ma, I'm road kill! Hahaha!"

"I meant what I said, and I said what I meant. An elephant's faithful, one-hundred percent."

"A person's a person, no matter how small."

"Why do I fall in love with every woman I see that shows me the least bit of attention?"

"All right, I'm late. I ran oughta gas! The gauge is broken. Rough neighborhood too. Good thing I was wearing neutral gang colors. Might've had to rip out my nine and bust a cap! My mind on my money and my money on my mind!"

"I could have died there on the street, but that wouldn't have been justice. At least not the justice fathers teach their sons."

"Love me. Love me."

"I'm very disappointed in you children."

"I thought this was a democracy."

"I saw it, and it was *goooood!*"

"Do not go in there! Pheeww!"

"And that concludes our broadcast day, click."

The Many Faces of Jim Carrey in Film

Batman Forever

Liar Liar

The Majestic

Bruce Almighty

Eternal Sunshine of the Spotless Mind

Fun With Dick and Jane

Yes Man

The Truman Show

Dumb & Dumber

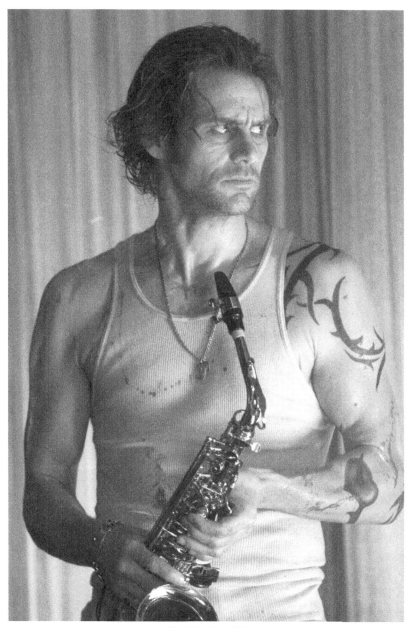

The Number 23

Lemony Snicket's A Series of Unfortunate Events

The Mask

Disney's A Christmas Carol

CHAPTER 11

Film Critics' and Fans' Reviews

These particular reviews focus more on the reviewer's take of Jim Carrey's performances rather than the films themselves.

What The Film Critics Said...

Ace Ventura: Pet Detective

"Carrey plays Ace as if he's being clocked on an Energy-O-Meter, and paid by the calories expended. He's a hyper goon who likes to screw his mouth into strange shapes while playing variations on the language. He shares his house with so many animals that he's like those zookeepers on late-night talk shows who always have pets crawling out of their collars. And he is simultaneously a spectacularly good and bad detective."—*The Chicago Sun Times*

The Mask

"Jim Carrey is at the height of funny in his role as Stanley Ipkis the bank teller. He totally lets loose when he puts on *The Mask*. Jim Carrey shines in this role—both as mild-mannered Stanley Ipkiss and as the love-crazy wildman, *The Mask.*" —*Movie Review Magazine*

"Mr. Carrey comes as close to being an animated creature as a live actor ever could. Add to that a goofy, ingenuous screen persona with obvious appeal for children and you have the not-so-surprising popularity of *Ace Ventura: Pet Detective*, the low-ball hit of the winter season."— *The New York Times*

Dumb and Dumber
"Mr. Carrey's version of Mr. Lewis, it should be noted, adds hefty dashes of sex and scatology in a six-year-old's style. The funniest scene in the movie involves a powerful laxative, a broken toilet and some graphically colorful sound effects."—*The New York Times*

Batman Forever
"Jim Carrey plays The Riddler and once he shows up, all the other actors might just as well go home. He burgles this picture out from under practiced scene-stealers Jones and Kilmer, both of whom are certainly good. You just don't notice them when Carrey is around."—*The Examiner*

"... The Riddler, played to the hilt by Jim Carrey in scene-stealing high gear. Mr. Carrey is the only performer in *Batman Forever* who is right in his element, frantically campy and reveling in wildly jokey effects. 'Caffeine 'il kill ya,' he exclaims, clobbering someone with a coffee pot. All dimples and insane glee, he can magically sap the malice out of a moment like that."—*The New York Times*

Ace Ventura: When Nature Calls

"Carrey is in excellent form, with razor-like observation and a pliant physicality that continues to defy the tenets of *Gray's Anatomy*. Though his manner echoes past clowns as diverse as Keaton and Jerry Lewis, no one has ventured out on the thin limb of taste to this extent without breaking a bough."—*Variety*

"Carrey is in top form here, giving a wildly confident, physically draining performance with all the stops pulled out."—*Austin Chronicles*

The Cable Guy

"... Carrey plunges into the demonic as a cable TV installer who can be your best friend or your worst enemy. He's brilliant at times, but mostly a turnoff as a guy who's always on."— *The San Francisco Chronicle*

Liar Liar

"Two little words: Jim Carrey. That's all it takes to transform *Liar Liar* from a formulaic Hollywood comedy into an uproarious one-man free-for-all."—*The New York Times*

The Truman Show

"Jim Carrey's instantly iconic performance as the sweet, unsuspecting Truman will give his career deserved new impetus, but the real star of *The Truman Show* is its premise."—*The New York Times*

"His gifts as a comic actor are well-known, but who would have thought that Jim Carrey might simultaneously break your heart as easily as he makes you laugh?... Carrey's trademark high-energy mania plays like the result of the unknowing artificiality of his life, precisely the way someone might get if everyone he knew was secretly more of a co-star than a friend." —*The Los Angeles Times*

Man On The Moon

"Carrey deserves an Oscar nomination for no other reason than we didn't think of *Ace Ventura* once."— *Maxim*

"...Mr. Carrey delivers an electrifying homage *in Man on the Moon*, Milos Forman's vivid re-creation of Kaufman's too-short and enduringly strange career."— *The New York Times*

"Jim Carrey does a meticulous job of re-creating the right mannerisms and body language, and a surprising amount of screen time is devoted to staging Kaufman's old bits— the Elvis impersonation, the wrestling and The Great Gatsby routine."—*San Francisco Chronicle*

"...Jim Carrey is brilliant in a role he was meant to play: the funny, sad, strange and subversive comedic genius of Andy Kaufman."—*Baltimore Sun*

Me, Myself & Irene

"As Hank, Mr. Carrey shows the edge of creepiness that made him so repellent, and so fascinating, in the underrated *Cable Guy*. It's a rare comedian who can be so completely repulsive and at the same time so lovable"—*The New York Times*

Dr. Seuss' How The Grinch Stole Christmas

"Mr. Carrey's wrinkled green-faced Grinch is relentless. Determined at all costs to be recognizable through his furry costume, the star regularly breaks character to address the camera and fire off smart-aleck remarks and references like 'dude' and 'faaabulous.'"—*The New York Times*

Disney's A Christmas Carol

"Carrey gets to be both his silly self and stretch his acting chops all without a drop of makeup; too bad the filmmakers could barely keep the camera still long enough to capture the performance rather than sweep the audience off their feet." —*Rottentomatoes.com*

The Majestic

"Anybody who thinks Carrey isn't capable of subtlety is in for a big surprise. At the same time, the movie pulls off the neat juggling act of paying tribute to a sense of wartime patriotism while making a defense of civil liberties."— *The San Francisco Chronicle*

"When Carrey breaks into an 'aw, shucks' smile, you can spot the maniacal trickster lurking beneath the bland demeanor that the part imposes on him."—*USA Today*

"If the neo-sentimental movie's good for anything, it's to prove there's more to Carrey than wild-eyed comedy. He can act."— *The Village Voice*

Bruce Almighty

"You could not ask for a better showcase for what Jim Carrey does best than this comedy about a man who is given all of God's powers and has no compunction about using them for cheap thrills and petty payback."—*Movie Mom Review*

"There is about Jim Carrey a desperate urgency that can be very funny, as he plunges with manic intensity after his needs and desires."—*The Chicago Sun Times*

Lemony Snicket's A Series of Unfortunate Events

"Carrey was born to play the part of Count Olaf, a master of bad disguise."—*Life and Style Weekly*

"As in all Jim Carrey's comic creations, the man occasionally pokes through the skin of the character(s) – in addition to Count Olaf, Carrey takes on the guise of a peg-legged sea captain and a fusty reptile expert. Carrey is a bit of a conundrum: He's the best and worst thing about *Lemony Snicket*."—*The Austin Chronicle*

Eternal Sunshine of the Spotless Mind

"Jim Carrey is a revelation in his toned-down and evocative performance. He has attempted weighty roles before — and he did a fine job as the enigmatic Andy Kaufman in *Man on the Moon*, but this is his finest effort to date."—*USA Today*

"The Jim Carrey on display here is not the rubber-faced, *alrighty-then* Carrey that the masses know and love. This is the art-film Carrey: repressed, lovesick, unshaven."—*The Boston Globe*

Fun With Dick and Jane

"Mr. Carrey's admirers may not mind the zigging and zagging, since he spends most of his screen time slaloming from one high jinx to the next, really misting up with actorly sentiment only once."— *The New York Times*

"... Carrey's previous forays into seriousness have given ballast to his lunatic physicality. Now when his body breaks down, his heart appears to follow."— *The Boston Globe*

The Number 23

"Alas, this great comic talent seems to think he's fronting a serious film, an assignment for which he has reined in his body, trading his ductile physicality and natural grace for moody stares and anguished postures that, in all likelihood, will soon be mirrored by even his more adamant fans in the audience."—*The Movie Forum*

"*The Number 23* makes good use of Carrey's glib but distant quality, that friendly but unknowable essence that hints at something tortured and out of control behind the smile."—*The San Francisco Chronicle*

"While you have got to admire Jim Carrey's desire to stretch beyond his *Dumb and Dumber* screen persona, opting to star in *The Number 23* about a guy who becomes obsessed with an omnipresent pair of digits is hardly a career-enhancing decision."—*The Palm Beach Post*

Horton Hears A Who

"Horton, given a comically innocent voice by Jim Carrey, is a rubbery elephant in the jungle of Nool who one fine day hears a tiny cry. It comes from a speck floating in the air, which actually is a tiny planet, home to a city called Who-ville, inhabited by microscopic denizens known as Whos."—*Hollywood Reporter*

"Horton (voiced charmingly by Jim Carrey) is a cheerful, big-hearted galoot of an elephant. One day as he's tromping through the jungle, he hears a distant sound that appears to be coming from a speck of dust."— *USA Today*

What The Fans Said...

The Number 23

"It's good to see Jim Carrey try some different. I am happy for him. So what if the movie critics didn't like it. I think like *Eternal Sunshine*, this is one of his better movies."

"I was surprised to see Jim Carrey put in one of the best performances he has done in years. I like seeing the edgy Jim. How can you not feel his character's relentless pain and hopeless obsession? I hope he does more movies like *The Number 23*."

"The ever clever Jim Carrey invented a new kind of work in films. He never ceases to impress us loyal fans. *The Number 23* is an interesting enough that it makes you question what the big secret is. You want his character to ultimately be all right and not to so crazy in his personal pain and obsession."

Fun With Dick And Jane

"What makes Jim Carrey so great in this film is that for once he doesn't over act in it. He is equally as believable as he is hilarious."

"Of all Jim Carrey's films, this *Fun With Dick and Jane* is my favorite. He's funny without being over the top. This is one of his best."

Eternal Sunshine of the Spotless Mind

"Bravo Jim Carrey! Finally a film where we can really see his true acting talents! So the movie's timeline is a bit confusing. So what, Jim's brilliant performance made me forget what I couldn't follow so well."

"I love Jim Carrey in this film because he's not playing the funny guy. His acting is remarkable. I couldn't have been more impressed. I hope he does more films like this in the future."

Lemony Snicket's A Series of Unfortunate Events

"Jim Carrey rocks in this film! He totally gets his character, the dark humor and all. Having read all three books, Jim's portrayal of Count Olaf did not disappoint."

"Jim Carrey is funny in a Tim Burton kind of way. It's a typical Jim Carrey movie in every way. He really pulls off an ace performance as Count Olaf. It's his best role since the Grinch."

Bruce Almighty

"I'm a huge Jim Carrey fan and can't say enough how amazing he is in this film. There is no comparison from his earlier films like *Ace Ventura* or *The Mask*. As an actor, he has come so far and is one of today's important comedic talents."

"Jim Carrey delivers yet another great performance in *Bruce Almighty*. But why would we think he would do anything less? Playing God is more than a big responsibility and he pulls it off just the right amount of humor and comedic timing. Just when I think Jim Carrey can't make me laugh anymore, he makes me laugh even harder."

The Majestic

"Jim Carrey is great in *The Majestic*. I think he gives the best performance of his career. He plays a very convincing romantic lead. Don't watch this film if you are looking for his wacky Ace Ventura or Mask characters. You will be disappointed. Watch *The Majestic* with an open mind and you won't be disappointed. Expect to see a serious Jim Carrey."

"Jim Carrey may play a B-movie screenwriter that gets amnesia, but he gives an unforgettable performance."

Dr. Suess' How The Grinch Stole Christmas

"Every time I see this film, I can't stop laughing. Jim Carrey really is The Grinch. No one else could play the part like him. He is brilliant!"

The Truman Show

"What a remarkable performance Jim Carrey gives in *The Truman Show*. He is such a natural. His talent never ceases to amaze me."

Liar Liar

"*Liar Liar is* one of the funniest films Jim Carrey has ever been in. His comedic timing as usual is perfect."

The Cable Guy

"This is one of Jim Carrey's best movies. Anyone can see how much he has grown as an actor. He is hilarious in *The Cable Guy*. I never get tired of watching this film."

"I can watch Jim Carrey in *The Cable Guy over and* over again, especially that great karaoke scene. Not many actors can sing as well as they act. Carrey has got that down pat."

Ace Ventura: When Nature Calls

"Jim Carrey is funny, but this film is no way as good as the first one, though the jokes were better than I expected. I'm a big fan of Jim, but I don't think he should do sequels."

"It must be true, Jim Carrey is made of rubber! I loved this film. He makes me laugh hard. He is just so funny, especially when he says those classics lines and we all know which ones they are!"

Batman Forever

"I never thought Jim Carrey could play such a convincing Riddler, but he does. It's not one of the best *Batman* movies out there, but Jim Carrey's performance is over the top."

Dumb And Dumber

"This is without a doubt, Jim Carrey at his very best. It's the funniest I've ever seen him."

The Mask

"*The Mask* is Jim Carrey's greatest movie performance. It's not just funny, and it's one of those movies you can see ten times or more and not get tired of it."

"Jim Carrey's performance in *The Mask* is his funniest ever. He is simply fabulous in the role. No one does it better!"

Ace Ventura: Pet Detective

"This is the absolute quintessential Jim Carrey movie of all time. He is one of the best actors of our time. No one could have played that part but Jimbo himself."

CHAPTER 12

Lesser-Known and Fun Facts on Jim Carrey

What sets Jim Carrey apart from the pack of Hollywood actors that started out at the same time is he is still a viable force in the film business today, while others have been relegated to the live comedy or television circuits. He's been making people laugh since he was a kid in Canada, putting on one-man shows for family and friends.

Fans were most surprised at the 2003 psycho-thriller *The Number 23*. Though it opened to most negative reviews, a few major film critics gave it a thumb's up, particularly KABC-TV in Los Angeles and Ebert & Roeper.

Did You Know? . . .

- Jim made his name in the US as a cast member of the hit TV show, *In Living Color*.

- At age 10, Jim sent his resume to Carol Burnett. Even then he was funny and wanted to be famous!

- Jim appeared at the 20th anniversary special for *The Comedy Store* wearing nothing but a sock covering his manhood, and to the MTV fashion awards wearing nothing but a fig leaf!

- It is well documented that Jim has received $20 million per film. However, if he is passionate about a film that has a lower budget, he will accept for far less.

- In the mid-'80, Jim co-hosted the YTV (Canadian Youth Television) Awards. Jim was just a teenager!

- Jim once dated Linda Ronstadt when he was 21 (she was 37!) He was the opening act on her concert tour.

- Jim was chosen in 1997 by *People* magazine as one of the 50 Most Beautiful People in the World.

- Jim has a 21-year-old daughter named Jane, from his first marriage with Melissa Womer.

- As a comedian and Jim has opened shows for singers Sheena Easton and Linda Ronstadt. He has also opened for comedians Rodney Dangerfield and Rich Little.

- One of Jim's good friends is actor Nicolas Cage (they met on the set of *Peggy Sue Got Married* in 1986).

- Jim was the lowest paid member of the troupe from the short-lived TV show *The Duck Factory*— $5000 per episode.

- The role of the Riddler in *Batman Forever* was originally offered to Robin Williams. Jim was offered the role *before* Robin Williams turned it down!

- The role of *The Cable Guy* was supposed to be por-

trayed by Chris Farley.   Once Jim was cast, his en-
tourage re-wrote the script into a dark comedy.   The
movie originally meant to be a lighter comedy.

- In 1998 Jim performed "Rocket Man" with Elton John
  at one of his concerts.

- Jim infuriated the cast and crew of The *Number 23*
  when he publicly urinated on one of the actual movie
  sets.

- Jim has been heralded "genius" by the French who re-
  fer to him as the son of Jerry Lewis.

- Jim auditioned for *Saturday Night Live* at the same time
  as Dana Carvey and Phil Hartman. He failed the audi-
  tion.

- While filming *Man on the Moon*, Jim suffered neck in-
  juries recreating the scene featuring professional wres-
  tler, Jerry Lawlor.

- In real life, Jim is an extremely private person who pre-
  fers to avoid the paparazzi.

- Jim shares the same birthday with Andy Kaufman, who
  he portrayed in *Man on the Moon.*

- For the *Ace Ventura: Pet Detective* soundtrack, Jim in-
  sisted that his favorite band at the time, Cannibal
  Corpse, be included on the album.

- Jim knows how to throw a party! He once rented
  the Six Flags theme park in Valencia, California to celebrate the release *of Fun with Dick and Jane.* Jim invited

over 500 guests including the film's cast and crew and their families. He rode one of the park's extreme roller coasters that included a 200-foot drop with his then 17-year-old daughter Jane. The cost of the six-hour Fun with Jim Carrey blast? Over $100,000.

- Jim dedicated his 1991 HBO special *Jim Carrey: The Un-Natural Act* to his mother who had died earlier that year.

- Jim was slated to play Willy Wonka, but it took 14 months to tell him he got the role and then it was too late—Jim had already begun filming *Fun with Dick and Jane.*

- James Stewart is one of Jim's heroes. When he got to meet the legendary actor in the 80s, Jim was so nervous that he said he made a fool of himself.

- In Canada, a booking agent who saw his stand up act discovered Jim. He gave Jim his first big break opening for legendary comedian Rodney Dangerfield in Las Vegas.

- Jim never finished high school. He went as far as the ninth grade.

- As a child Jim loved to gain attention by clowning for family and friends.

- In 1981, Jim became a regular performer at Mitzi Shore's Comedy Store in Los Angeles.

- In 2004 Jim has become public about his bouts with depression.

- Jim recorded "I Am the Walrus" on the George Martin tribute album *In My Life*.

- Prior to his Hollywood stardom, Jim was known as "the white guy" on *In Living Color*.

- By age 19, Jim became Toronto's hot young comic of the day, where he earned $40,000 for a three-night stand.

- Jim decided in 1987 to drop impressions and impersonations from his stand up routines.

- In the TV film, *Doing Time On Maple Drive*, Jim played a serious role as a troubled alcoholic teen.

- In 2005, Jim began dating Jenny McCarthy, but as of late 2007 has no plans to marry again.

- When he was only 10 years, Jim tried to get a book of his poems published.

- Jim landed parts in the two Clint Eastwood films, *The Dead Pool* (1988) and *Pink Cadillac* (1989). Eastwood rallied for Jim to take these parts after seeing his impression of him.

- Jim helped pen the script for *Ace Ventura: Pet Detective*.

- Jim once wrote a song for the acoustic duo Tuck and Patti.

- Jim cites Dick Van Dyke, Jerry Lewis, Mel Brooks and Bill Cosby as some of his early comedic influences.

- Jim made his film debut in *Rubber Face* (1983), which was later re-titled *Introducing ... Janet*.

- Jim appeared on *Saturday Night Live* as a Jacuzzi Life Guard.

- Jim once pretended to be arrested by New York City police during a taping of the *Late Show with David Letterman*.

- Known to go to extremes when preparing for a role, Jim shaved his head for *Lemony Snicket*.

- Jim appeared in a straight-to-YouTube video campaigning the release of Aung San Suu Kyi , the world's only detained Noble Peace prize winner.

CHAPTER 13

Web Sites

There are literally hundreds of Jim Carrey web sites, newsgroups, blogs, etc., that exist on the Internet. Listed here are some of the more highly rated ones (both official and unofficial) preferred by Carrey fans worldwide. Please note that the URLs for Internet web sites frequently change.

Official Movie Sites

Man on the Moon
www.universalpictures.com/manonthemoon/

The Majestic
http://majesticmovie.warnerbros.com

Bruce Almighty
www.brucealmighty.com

Eternal Sunshine of the Spotless Mind
www.eternalsunshineofthespotlessmind.com • www.lacunainc.com

Fun With Dick and Jane
www.sonypictures.com/movies/funwithdickandjane/site

Horton Hears a Who
www.hortonmovie.com

Yes Man
www.yesisthenewno.warnerbros.com

Disney's a Christmas Carol
www.disney.go.com/disneypictures/achristmascarol

Other Film-Related Websites

IMDB (Internet Film Database)
www.imdb.com

Cinema.com
www.cinema.com

Movie Web
www.movieweb.com

Star Pulse
www.starpulse.com

Thespian Net
www.thespiannet.com

Yahoo Movies
http://movies.yahoo.com

Moviefone
http://movies.aol.com

Film Spot
www.filmspot.com

Movie Centre
www.moviecentre.net

Only Official Website

www.jimcarrey.com

#1 Rated Fan Site

Jim Carrey Online
www.jimcarreyonline.com
www.myspace.com/jimcarreyonline
www.facebook.com/jimcarreyonline
www.youtube.com/jimcarreyonline
www.twitter.com/jimcarreyonline

Select Fan Websites (in no particular order)

Jim Carrey World
www.jimcarreyworld.com

Jim Carrey Fan Site
www.angelfire.com/celeb2/jimcarreyfan/index02.html

Jim Almighty
http://totally-random.net/jim/

See Fansites.com for additional Jim Carrey fan pages that include abbreviated biographies, wallpapers, discussions, photos, facts, rumors, and where to buy autographs, movie posters and other memorabilia.

Current News, Biographies, Blogs, Message Boards and other Miscellaneous Information

AskMen
www.askmen.com

Wikipedia
www.wikipedia.org/

MTV
www.mtv.com

Rolling Stone
www.rollingstone.com

People Magazine
www.people.com

Rotten Tomatoes
www.rottentomatoes.com

New York Times Movies
www.movies.nytimes.com

E! News
www.eonline.com

Variety
www.variety.com

The Hollywood Reporter
www.hollywoodreporter.com

Celebrity Pro
www.celebritypro.com

Fox News
www.foxnews.com

Contact Music
www.contactmusic.com

Topix
www.topix.net/who/jim-carrey

Celebrity Pro
www.celebritypro.com/jim_carrey

At Pictures
www.atpictures.com/jim/

Celebs We Love
www.celebwelove.com

CelebrityWonder
www.celebritywonder.com

Holly Scoop
www.Hollyscoop.com

Absolute Now
www.absolute.com

Celebrity Genius
www.celebritygenius.com

Perfect People
www.perfectpeople.net

Movie Stills

Americola—Celebrity Pop Culture
www.americola.com/sites/Jim+Carrey/

AllMegaStar
www.allmegastar.com/c/JimCarrey

Hotflick
www.hotflick.net/celebs/jim_carrey.html

On TV and Video

TV Now
www.tv-now

TV Guide
www.tvguide.com/celebrities/jim-carrey/157028

You Tube
www.YouTube.com

My Space
www.myspace.com

Part 3

Appendix 1

(Select) Television Appearances— Including Guest Star and Episodic, and Recommended Reading (1984–2009).

1984
The Duck Factory, NBC
Jerry Lewis Week: Buffalo Bill, NBC

1986
The Bob Monkhouse Show, BBC

1990-94
In Living Color, Fox

1991
Jim Carrey: The Un-Natural Act, Showtime
Late Show With David Letterman, CBS
The Tonight Show Starring Johnny Carson, NBC
Tom Arnold: The Naked Truth, HBO

1992
The Comedy Store's 20th Birthday, NBC
Comic Relief V, HBO
The Dennis Miller Show, syndicated
Sesame Street, PBS

1993
A Tribute To Sam Kinison, Fox
The Tonight Show Starring Johnny Carson
The Mask: Space Ghost Coast To Coast, Cartoon Network
The Howard Stern Show, syndicated
Late Show With David Letterman, CBS

1994
Dennis Miller Live, syndicated
Late Show With David Letterman, CBS
Space Ghost Coast To Coast, Cartoon Network
The Howard Stern Show, E!

1995
The Barbra Walters Special, ABC
Comedy Central Spotlight: Jim Carrey, Comedy Central
A Comedy Salute to Andy Kaufman, NBC
Riddle Me This: Why is Batman Forever?, ABC
Canned Ham: The Cable Guy, Comedy Central
Le livre d'histoire: Space Gost Coast to Coast, Cartoon Network
Space Ghost Coast to Coast, Cartoon Network
Showbiz Today, CNN
The Tonight Show With Jay Leno, NBC
Show Biz Today, CNN

1996

The Mask (A Comedy of Eras episode)
The Life and Death of Sam Kinison: The E! True Hollywood Story, E!
Saturday Night Live, NBC

1998

In My Life, Bravo
The Larry Sanders Show, HBO
The Oprah Winfrey Show, syndicated
The Entertainment Business, Bravo
Flip, The Larry Sanders Show, HBO
Rodney Dangerfield: Respect at Last, A&E Biography

1999

AFI's 100 Years... 100 Stars, CBS
Andy Kaufman's Really Big Show, A&E
Larry King Live, CNN
Nicolas Cage: Wild at Heart, A&E Biography
The Tonight Show With Conan O'Brien, CBS
Late Show With David Letterman, CBS

2000

AFI's 100 Years, 100 Laughs: America's Funniest Movies, CBS
Larry King Live, CNN
Canned Ham: Me, Myself & Irene, Comedy Central
The Rosie O'Donnell Show, ABC
Life and Times, CBC

2001

HBO First Look, HBO
The Rosie O'Donnell Show, ABC
The Charlie Rose Show, PBS
America: A Tribute To Heroes
Concert For New York City
Comedy Store: The E! Hollywood Story, E!
Hollywood Salutes Nicolas Cage

2002

An American Cinematheque Tribute
Appeared in Various *MTV* Specials throughout the year
Super Market Sweep, ABC

2003

Saturday Night Live, NBC
The Tonight Show With Jay Leno, NBC
The Oprah Winfrey Show, syndicated
Late Show With David Letterman, CBS
Revealed With Jules Asner, E!
Late Night with Conan O'Brien, CBS
Howard Stern Show, E!
Friday Night with Jonathan Ross, BBC
Enough Rope with Andrew Denton, ABC
Celebrities Uncensored, E!
Richard & Judy, Channel 4
The Oprah Winfrey Show, syndicated

2004

The Wayne Brady Show, ABC
The Oprah Winfrey Show, syndicated
Late Night with Conan O'Brien, CBS
Tinseltown TV
On Air with Ryan Seacrest, syndicated
Late Show with David Letterman, CBS
The Ellen DeGeneres Show, syndicated
T4, BBC
GMTV, iTV
Larry King Live, CNN
Total Request Live, MTV
Live With Regis and Kathie Lee, ABC
Only In LA, syndication

2005

The Oprah Winfrey Show, syndicated
The Insider, syndicated
Entertainment Tonight, CBS
Extra, NBC
The Ellen DeGeneres Show, syndicated
Late Show with David Letterman, CBS
The Today Show, NBC
Late Night with Conan O'Brien, CBS
The Early Show, CBS
Film 72, BBC

2006

GMTV, iTV

2007

The Tonight Show With Jay Leno, NBC
Extra, NBC
TV Guide Close Up, TVGC
Late Show with David Letterman, CBS
The Today Show, NBC
Total Request Live, MTV
Late Night with Conan O'Brien, NBC
The View, ABC

2008

The Oprah Winfrey Show, syndicated
The Today Show, NBC
The Tonight Show With Jay Leno, NBC
Live With Regis and Kelly, ABC
Entertainment Tonight, CBS
Late Night With David Letterman, CBS
American Idol, ABC
The Ellen Degeneres Show, syndicated
Jimmy Kimmel Live!, syndicated
Good Morning America, ABC

2009

Entertainment Tonight,CBS
The Ellen Degeneres Show, syndicated
Kid's Choice Awards, Nickelodeon
Larry King Live, CNN
The Tonight Show with Conan O'Brien, NBC
MTV Movie Awards, MTV
Good Morning America, ABC

Select Books on and/or Relating to Jim Carrey

Here listed are selected American-, Canadian- and United Kingdom-published books on Jim Carrey. For over a decade more than twenty books — hard covers, soft covers and a handful of mass-market paperbacks — have been published on Jim Carrey. Several of these books are now officially out-of-print, but are still available through the Internet and used bookstores.

Batman Forever: the Official Movie Book (Modern Publishing, 1995)

Jim Carrey: Comic Ace by Deborah G. Felder (Random House, 1995)

Jim Carrey: Unmasked by Roy Trakin (St. Martin's Press, 1995)

Behind The Scenes With Jim Carrey (Trumpet Club Press, 1995)

Jim Carrey Funny Man (Reaching For the Stars) by Joan Wallner (Abdo Publishing Company, 1996)

Jim Carrey (Taking Part) by Paul Guzetti (Dillion Press, 1997)

Jim Carrey by Paula Guzzetti (Dillion Press, 1998)

Jim Carrey: Overcoming Adversity by Mary Hughes (Chelsea House, 1998)

Andy Kaufman Revealed! Best Friend Tells All by Bob Zmuda, Matthew Scott Hansen, Jim Carrey (Little Brown & Company, 1999)

Jim Carrey by Mary Hughes (Chelsea House, 1999)

Jim Carrey by John F. Wukovits (Lucent Books 1999)

The Joker is Wild: the Trials of Triumphs of Jim Carrey by Martin Knelman (penguin Putman, 1999)

Jim Carrey (People in the News) by John F. Wukovits (Greehaven Press, 1999)

Jim Carrey: The Joker is Wild by Martin Knelman (Firefly Books, 1999)

Jim Carrey by Martin Knelman (Blake Publishing. 2000)

The Jim Carrey Scrapbook by Ed Scott (Citadel Publishing, 2000)

Jim Carrey: Fun and Funnier by Nancy Krulik (Tandem Library, 2000)

Jim Carrey by Jill C. Wheeler (Addo Publishers, 2001)

Jim Carrey: Star Tracks by Jill C. Wheeler (ABDO & Daughters Publishers, 2002)

Jim Carrey Today's Superstars: Entertainment (Gareth Stevens Publishing, 2007)

Select Film Script, Adaptation and Novelization Books

Dumb and Dumber by Madeline Dorr (Troll Communications, 1994)

Batman Forever: The Novelization by Peter David, Janet Scott Batchler (Warner Books, 1995)

Batman Forever by Alan Grant (Little Brown & Company, 1995)

Ace Ventura: Pet Detective (Movie Novelization) by Marc Cerashi (Random House For Young Readers, 1995)

Ace Ventura: Pet Detective by Marc Cerasini (Random House, 1995)

Ace Ventura: When Nature Calls by Marc Berstnstein (Bullseye Books, 1995)

Ace Ventura: When Nature Calls by Steve Oedekerk (Scholastic, 1996)

Ace Ventura: When Nature Calls by Marc A. Cerashi (Random House, 1996)

The Cable Guy by Harriet Grey (St. Martin's Press, 1996)

The Truman Show: Shooting Script by Adrew Niccoli and Peter Weir (Newmarket Press, 1998)

Me, Myself & Irene: A Novel by David Jacobs (St. Martin's Press, 2000)

The Truman Show (Klett, 2002)

Eternal Sunshine of the Spotless Mind: The Shooting Script (Newmarket Shooting Script Series) by Charlie Kaufman and Michel Gondry (Newmarket Press, 2004)

Eternal Sunshine of the Spotless Mind by Charlie Kaufman and Michel Gondry (Nick Hern Books, 2004)

Charlie Kaufman Shooting Script Set, Collection 2: Eternal Sunshine of the Spotless Mind and Adaptation by Charlie Kaufman (New Market Press. 2005)

Lemony Snicket's A Series of Unfortuate Events (HarperCollins, 2004)

Art of A Christmas Carol by Diana Landau (Disney Editions, 2009)

Appendix 2
Select Awards Won (1995–2010)

1995

London Critics Circle Film Awards (ALFS) Award
   Category: Newcomer of the Year for The Mask (1994)

Blimp Award (Kid's Choice Award)
   Category: Favorite Movie Actor for Ace Ventura: Pet Detective (1994)

MTV Movie Awards
   Category: Best Actor for Dumb and Dumber (1994)

MTV Movie Awards
   Category: Best Kiss for Dumb and Dumber (1994), shared with Lauren Holly

MTV Movie Award
   Category: Best Dance Sequence for The Mask (1994)

ShoWest Special Award (ShoWest Convention)
   Category: Comedy Star of the Year

MTV Movie Award
   Category: Best Comedic Performance for Dumb & Dumber (1994)

Blockbuster Entertainment Award
> *Category: Favorite Male Newcomer On Video for Ace Ventura: Pet Detective (1994)*

Blockbuster Entertainment Award
> *Category: Favorite Movie Actor - Comedy On Video for Ace Ventura: Pet Detective (1994)*

1996

MTV Movie Award
> Category: Best Male Performance for *Ace Ventura: When Nature Calls* (1995)

MTV Movie Award
> Category: Best Comedic Performance for *Ace Ventura: When Nature Calls* (1995)

Blimp Award (Kid's Choice Award)
> Category: Favorite Movie Actor for *Ace Ventura: When Nature Calls* (1995)

1997

MTV Movie Award
> *Category: Best Comedic Performance for Ace Ventura: When Nature Calls (1995)*

MTV Movie Award
> *Category: Best Male Performance for Ace Ventura: When Nature Calls (1995)*

MTV Movie Award
> *Category: Best Villain for The Cable Guy (1996)*

Blimp Award (Kid's Choice Award)
> *Category: Favorite Movie Actor for The Cable Guy (1996)*

MTV Movie Award
> *Category: Best Comedic Performance for The Cable Guy (1996)*

1998

MTV Movie Award
> *Category: Best Comedic Performance for Liar Liar (1997)*

Blockbuster Entertainment Award
> *Category: Favorite Actor - Comedy for Liar Liar (1997)*

1999

Grace Award
> *Category: The Truman Show (1998)*

MTV Movie Award
> *Category: Best Male Performance for The Truman Show (1998)*

Golden Globe
> *Category: Best Performance by an Actor in a Motion Picture - Drama for The Truman Show (1998)*

Boston Society of Film Critics (BSFC) Award
> *Category: Best Actor for Man on the Moon (1999)*

2000

Golden Globe
> *Category: Best Performance by an Actor in a Motion Picture - Comedy/Musical for Man on the Moon (1999)*

Teen Choice Award
>   Category: Film - Wipeout Scene of the Summer for Me, Myself &
>   Irene (2000)

ShoWest Award (ShoWest Convention)
>   Category: Male Star of the Year

Received a star on The Hollywood Walk of Fame

2001

Blimp Award (Kid's Choice Award)
>   Category: Favorite Movie Actor for How the Grinch Stole Christmas
>   (2000)

Teen Choice Award
>   Category: Film - Choice Hissy Fit for How the Grinch Stole Christmas
>   (2000)

People's Choice Award
>   Category: Favorite Motion Picture Star in a Comedy

Nickelodeon Kid Choice Award
>   Category: Best Actor for How the Grinch Stole Christmas (2000)

MTV Movie Award
>   Category: Best Villain for How the Grinch Stole Christmas (2000)

Blockbuster Entertainment Award
>   Category: Favorite Actor - Comedy for How the Grinch Stole Christ-
>   mas (2000)

2003

Teen Choice Award
> Category: Choice Movie Actor - Comedy for Bruce Almighty (2003)

2004

Blimp Award (Kid's Choice Award)
> Category: Favorite Movie Actor for Bruce Almighty (2003)

San Diego Film Awards (SDFCS) Award
> Category: Best Actor for Eternal Sunshine of the Spotless Mind
> (2004)

Nickeloden's Kid Choice Awards
> Category: Best Comedic Performance for Bruce Almighty (2003)

MTV Movie Awards, Mexico
> Category: Most Divine Miracle in a Movie for Bruce Almighty (2003)

Canadian Walk of Fame

2005

Teen Choice Award
> Category: Choice Movie Bad Guy for Lemony Snicket's A Series of
> Unfortunate Events (2004)

AFI Award (U.S. Comedy Arts Festival)

2006

MTV Generation Award

Teen Choice Award
> *Category: Choice Movie Bad Guy for Lemony Snicket's A Series of Unfortunate Events (2004)*

2009

MTV Movie Award
> *Category: Best Comedic Performance for Yes Man (2008)*

2010

People's Choice Award
> *Category: Favorite Comedic Star*

Blimp Award (Kids' Choice Awards)
> *Category: Favorite Voice From An Animated Movie for A Christmas Carol (2009)*

Select Nominations

1994

MTV Movie Award
> *Category: Best Comedic Performance for Ace Ventura: Pet Detective (1994)*

1995

Golden Globe
> Category: Best Performance by an Actor in a Motion Picture - Comedy/Musical for The Mask (1994)

MTV Movie Award
> Category: Best Comedic Performance for The Mask (1994)

MTV Movie Award
> Category: Best Dance Sequence for The Mask (1994), shared with Cameron Diaz

MTV Movie Award
> Category: Best On-Screen Duo for Dumb & Dumber (1994), shared with Jeff Daniels

Razzie Award
> Category: Worst New Star for Ace Ventura: Pet Detective (1994)

1996

MTV Movie Award
> Category: Best Villain for Batman Forever (1995)

MTV Movie Award
> Category: Best Kiss for Ace Ventura: When Nature Calls (1995) shared with Sophie Okonedo

American Comedy Award
> Category: Funniest Actor in a Motion Picture (Leading Role) for Ace Ventura: When Nature Calls (1995)

American Comedy Award
> *Category: Funniest Actor in a Motion Picture (Leading Role) for Ace Ventura: When Nature Calls (1995)*

1997

MTV Movie Award
> *Category: Best Fight (medieval time fight between Carrey and Matthew Broderick) for The Cable Guy (1996) shared with Broderick*

1998

Blimp Award (Kid's Choice Award)
> *Category: Favorite Movie Actor for Liar Liar (1997)*

Golden Globe
> *Category: Best Performance by an Actor in a Motion Picture - Comedy/Musical for Liar Liar (1997)*

CFCA (Chicago Film Critics Association) Award
Category: Best Actor for The Truman Show (1998)

1999

Blockbuster Entertainment Award
> *Category: Favorite Actor, Drama for The Truman Show (1998)*

American Comedy Award
> *Category: Funniest Male Guest Appearance in a TV Series for The Larry Sanders Show (1992) (TV)*

American Comedy Award
> *Category Funniest Actor in a Motion Picture (Leading Role) for The Truman Show (1998)*

Blimp Award (Kid's Choice Award)
> *Category: Favorite Movie Actor for The Truman Show (1998)*

Saturn Award (Academy of Science Fiction, Fantasy & Horror Films, USA)
> *Category: Best Actor for The Truman Show (1998)*

Canadian Comedy Award
> *Category: Film - Performance - Male for Man on the Moon (1999)*

MTV Movie Award
> *Category: Best Male Performance for Man on the Moon (1999)*

2000

MTV Movie Award
> *Category: Best Male Performance for Man on the Moon (1999)*

American Comedy Award
> *Category: Funniest Actor in a Motion Picture (Leading Role) for Man on the Moon (1999)*

OFCS Award (Online Film Critics Society Award)
> *Category: Best Actor for Man on the Moon (1999)*

Screen Actor's Guild Award
> *Category: Outstanding Performance by a Male Actor in a Leading Role for Man on the Moon (1999)*

Golden Satellite Award
> *Category: Best Performance by an Actor in a Motion Picture, Comedy or Musical for Man on the Moon (1999)*

Canadian Comedy Award
> *Category Film - Pretty Funny Male Performance for How the Grinch Stole Christmas (2000)*

2001

Empire Award (United Kingdom)
    Category: Best Actor for How the Grinch Stole Christmas (2000)

Golden Globe
    Category: Best Performance by an Actor in a Motion Picture - Comedy/Musical for How the Grinch Stole Christmas (2000)

Saturn Award (Academy of Science Fiction, Fantasy & Horror Films, USA)
    Category: Best Actor for How the Grinch Stole Christmas (2000)

Blockbuster Entertainment Award
    Category: Favorite Actor - Comedy/Romance for Me, Myself & Irene (2000)

ALFS Award (London Critics Circle Award)Category: Actor of the Year for How the Grinch Stole Christmas (2000)

MTV Movie Award
    Category: Best Comedic Performance for Me, Myself & Irene (2000)

2003

Teen Choice Award
    Category: Choice Movie Chemistry for Bruce Almighty (2003) shared with Morgan Freeman

2004

Teen Choice Award
    Category: Choice Comedian

TV Land Award
> *Category: Big Star/Little Screen Favorite*

MTV Movie Award
> *Category: Best Comedic Performance for Bruce Almighty (2003)*

MTV Movie Award
> *Category: Best Kiss for Bruce Almighty (2003), shared with Jennifer Aniston*

2005

People's Choice Award
> *Category: Favorite On-Screen Chemistry for Eternal Sunshine of the Spotless Mind (2004), shared with Kate Winslet*

Saturn Award (Academy of Science Fiction, Fantasy, & Horroe Films, USA)
> *Category: Best Actor for Eternal Sunshine of the Spotless Mind (2004)*

Teen Choice Award
> *Category: Choice Movie Liar for Lemony Snicket's A Series of Unfortunate Events (2004)*

Teen Choice Award
> *Category: Choice Comedian*

Teen Choice Award
> *Category: Choice Movie Actor: Action/Adventure/Thriller for Lemony Snicket's A Series of Unfortunate Events (2004)*

People's Choice Award
> *Category: Favorite Leading Man*

MTV Movie Award
>   Category: Best Villain for Lemony Snicket's A Series of Unfortunate Events (2004)

BAFTA Film Award
>   Category: Best Performance by an Actor in a Leading Role for Eternal Sunshine of the Spotless Mind (2004)

Golden Satellite Award
>   Category: Best Actor in a Motion Picture, Comedy or Musical for Eternal Sunshine of the Spotless Mind (2004)

OFCS Award (Online Film Critics Society Award)
>   Category: Best Actor for Eternal Sunshine of the Spotless Mind (2004)

Blimp Award (Kid's Choice Award)
>   Category: Favorite Movie Actor for Lemony Snicket's A Series of Unfortunate Events (2004)

Golden Globe
>   Category: Best Performance by an Actor in a Motion Picture - Musical or Comedy for Eternal Sunshine of the Spotless Mind (2004)

Empire Award (United Kingdom)
>   Category: Best Actor for Eternal Sunshine of the Spotless Mind (2004)

2006

Teen Choice Award
>   Category: Movies - Choice Actor: Comedy for Fun with Dick and Jane (2005)

Teen Choice Award
> Category: Choice Comedian

Blimp Award (Kid's Choice Awards)
> Category: Favorite Movie Actor for Fun with Dick and Jane (2005)

Moviefone Movie Goers Award
> Category: Most Hysterical Performance for Fun with Dick and Jane (2005)

2007

Teen Choice Award
> Category: Movies - Choice Movie Actor: Horror/Thriller for The Number 23 (2007)

2009

Teen Choice Award
> Category: Choice Movie Actor: Comedy for Yes Man (2008)

Teen Choice Awards
> Category: Choice Movie Hissy Fit for Yes Man" (2008)

Teen Choice Award
> Category: Choice Movie Rock Star Moment for Yes Man (2008)

2010

American Comedy Award
> Category: Category: Favorite Comedic Star

Blimp Award (Kids' Choice Awards)
> Category: Favorite Voice From An Animated Movie for A Christmas Carol (2009)

Appendix 3

Filmography
As Actor (Television and Film)

1981

*Introducing Janet (minor role; made for television). Released on video as
Rubber Face. Directors: Glen Salzman and Rebecca Yates*

1982

*Copper Mountain (featured role; made for television). Director: David
Mitchell*

1983

All In Good Taste (co-starring role). Director: Anthony Kramreither

1984

Finders Keepers (featured role). Director: Richard Lester

1985

Once Bitten (leading role). Director: Howard Storm

1986

Peggy Sue Got Married (supporting role). Director: Francis Coppola

1988

The Dead Pool (supporting role). Director: Buddy Van Horn

1989

Earth Girls Are Easy (leading role). Director: Jullien Temple

Mike Hammer: Murder Takes All (co-starring role). Director: John Nicolella

1991

High Strung (cameo appearance). Director: Roger Nygard

1992

Doing Time On Maple Drive (leading role; made for television). Director: Ken Olin

1994

Ace Ventura, Pet Detective (starring role). Director: Tim Shadyac

The Mask (starring role). Director: Charles Russell

Dumb and Dumber (starring role). Director: Peter Farrelly

1995

Batman Forever (featured role). Director: Joel Schumacher

Ace Ventura: When Nature Calls (starring role). Director: Steve Oedekerk

1996

The Cable Guy (starring role). Director: Ben Stiller

1997

Liar Liar (starring role). Director: Tom Shadyac

1998

The Truman Show (starring role). Director: Peter Weir

Simon Birch (cameo appearance). Director: Mark Steven Johnson

1999

Man on the Moon (starring role). Director: Milos Forman

2000

Me, Myself and Irene (starring role). Director: Peter Farrelly

How the Grinch Stole Christmas (starring role). Director: Ron Howard

2001

The Majestic (starring role). Director: Frank Darabont

2003

Bruce Almighty (starring role). *Director: Tom Shadyac*

2004

Lemony Snicket's A Series of Unfortunate Events (starring role). *Director: Brad Silberling*

Eternal Sunshine of the Spotless Mind (starring role). *Director: Michel Gondry*

2005

Fun With Dick and Jane (starring role). *Director: Dean Parisot*

2007

The Number 23 (starring role). *Director: Joel Schumacher*

2008

Horton Hears A Who (starring voice over role). *Directors: Jimmy Hayward, Steve Martino*

Yes Man (starring role). *Director: Payton Reed*

2009

A Christmas Carol (starring role). *Director: Robert Zemeckis*

Under the Sea 3D (Narrator)

As Producer (Television and Film)

Jim Carrey: The Un-Natural Act

Bruce Almighty

Fun With Dick and Jane

As Writer (Television and Film)

In Living Color

Jim Carrey: The Un-Natural Act

Ace Ventura: Pet Detective

Laughing Out Loud: America's Funniest Comedians

Carrey Movie Character Names

Introducing Janet/aka Rubber Face (1983). Character: Tony Moroni

Copper Mountain/aka A Club Med Experience (1983). Character: Bobby Todd

All in Good Taste (1983). Character: Ralph

Finders Keepers (1984). Character: Lane Bidlekoff

Once Bitten (1985). Character: Mark Kendall

Peggy Sue Got Married (1986). Character: Walter Getz

The Dead Pool (1988). Credited as James Carrey. Aka Dirty Harry (USA poster title. Character: Johnny Squares

Earth Girls Are Easy (1988). Character: Wiploc

Mike Hammer: Murder Takes All (1989). Character: Brad Peters

Pink Cadillac (1989). Credited as James Carrey. Character: Lounge Entertainer

High Strung (1991). Uncredited. Alternative title: Pissed Off. Character: Death.

The Itsy Bitsy Spider (1992). Animated. (Voice as James Carrey). Character: The   Exterminator

Doing Time on Maple Drive/aka Faces in The Mirror.(1992). Character: Tim Carter

The Mask (1994). Character: Stanley Ipkiss

Dumb & Dumber (1994). Character: Lloyd Christmas

Batman Forever (1995). Character: The Riddler/Edward Nygma

Ace Ventura: When Nature Calls (1995). Character: Ace Ventura

The Cable Guy (1996). Character: The Cable Guy

Liar Liar (1997). Character: Fletcher Reede.

The Truman Show (1998). Character: Truman Burbank

Sinon Birch/aka Angels and Armadilos (1998). Character: Adult Joe Wentworth

Man on the Moon (1999). Character: Andy Kaufman

Me, Myself & Irene (2000). Character: Officer Charlie Bailygates/Hank Evans

Dr. Seuss' How The Grinch Stole Christmas (2000). Character: The Grinch

The Majestic (2001). Character: Peter Appelton

Pecan Pie (2003). Character: The driver

Bruce Almighty (2003). Character: Bruce Nolan

Eternal Sunshine of the Spotless Mind (2004). Character: Joel Barish

Lemony Snicket's A Series of Unfortunate Events (2004). Character: Count Olaf

Fun With Dick and Jane (2005). Character: Dick Harper

The Number 23 (2007). Character: Walter Sparrow/Fingerling

Horton Hears a Who (2008). (Voice). Character: Horton

Yes Man (2008). Character: Carl Allen

I Love You Phillip Morris (2009). Character: Steven Russell

A Christmas Carol (2009). Characters: Ebenezer Scrooge / Ghost of Christmas Past / Ghost of Christmas Present / Ghost of Christmas Yet To Come /Scrooge as a young boy/Scrooge as a Teenage Boy/Scrooge as a Middle-aged Man

Sources

Information for this book has been obtained from various sources including press media kits from Paramount Pictures, New Line Cinema, 20th Century Fox, Warner Brothers, Universal Pictures Sony Pictures, Castle Rock Entertainment, Walt Disney Films, and Fox Network.

The author also used her own published stories and press conference material as well as from entertainment journalists, and industry insiders indirectly involved with Jim Carrey. This book was not by any means authorized or sponsored by Jim Carrey.

Magazines and Newspapers:

Variety, Hollywood Reporter, USA Today, People, Rolling Stone, Time, Entertainment Weekly, Newsweek, ABC News, Cahners Business, The New York Times, The Los Angeles Times, The Chicago Sun Times, The Atlanta Journal, Movie Review Magazine, The Washington Post, The Examiner, Austin Chronicles, The San Francisco Chronicle, The Film Critic, The Village Voice, Movie Mom Review, Life and Style Weekly, The Austin Chronicle, The Boston Globe, The Palm Beach Post, Current Biography,Gener8, Maxim. American Cinematographer, Life Story, Newsweek, Reader's Digest, Life Story, Esquire, Details, Premiere, Us Weekly, Parade, OK!, Rolling Stone,GQ, In Touch, USA Weekend, The New York Daily News, The New York Post

Websites:

Jimcarreyonline.com, boxofficereport.com, aceshowbiz.com, about.com, northernstars.com netflix.com,starwares.com, starpulse.com, epinions. com, uselessmoviequotes.com,nndb.com, movieworld.com, hollywood. com, topsites.com, fansites.com, jimcarreyworld.com, askmen.com, rottentomatoes.com, universalpictures.com, foxhome.com, warnerbros.com, brucealmighty,com, eternalsunhine.com, sonypictures.com, newline.com, hortonmovie.com, cinema.com, movieweb.com, thespiannet.com, movies.yahoo.com, movies.aol.com,filmspot.com, moviecentre.com, jimcarreywebsite. com,celebritieswelove.com, tvnow.com, tvguide.com, Wikipedia.com

Books

Jim Carrey: Fun and Funnier by Nancy Krulik (Pocket Books)
Jim Carrey: People in the News by John Wukovits (Lucent Books)
Jim Carrey: The Joker Is Wild by Martin Knelman (Firefly Books)
Jim Carrey: Overcoming Adversity

Photo Credits:

Unless noted, Universal Columbia Pictures, Paramount Pictures, Warner Bros. Pictures, New Line Cinema, Tri_Star, 20th Century Fox, Sony Pictures, Castle Rock, Fox Network, and Walt Disney Films.

Every effort has been to identify the copyright owners of the pictures used in this publication. The author and publisher apologize for any omissions and will make all necessary corrections in future editions.

About The Author

M.A. Cassata is the author of several entertainment-oriented books including *The Elton John Scrapbook* and *The Cher Scrapbook*. She is also the editorial director of *Faces Presents, Teen Dream* and *Word Up!*, three longstanding entertainment/teen magazines. Her two entertainment websites are: TheMACWIRE.com and OntheTEENBEAT.com.

Lightning Source UK Ltd.
Milton Keynes UK
UKOW07f2129261114

242250UK00019B/943/P